GEORGES MELIES
FATHER OF FILM FANTASY

DAVID ROBINSON

PUBLISHED IN CONJUNCTION WITH THE EXHIBITION 'GEORGES MELIES FATHER OF FILM FANTASY'
HELD AT THE MUSEUM OF THE MOVING IMAGE, 1993

INTRODUCTION

This little book is intended as an introduction to the life and work of Georges Méliès, who was a towering figure in the first decade of the cinema, and one of the most original and charming artists in the whole history of the film.

If, at the same time, it contributes something new to the considerable literature – mostly in French – on Méliès, it may be its attempt to identify and discard some of the accumulation of myth which Méliès' colourful career has inevitably attracted in the six decades since his death. There may also be new clues to the influence, upon his tastes and future, of the year he spent in London in 1884, at the age of 20.

As essential – and rewarding – further reading in English, John Frazer's Artificially Arranged Scenes (p) is particularly recommended for its survey of the atmosphere and culture which Méliès absorbed in late 19th century Paris; and Paul Hammond's Marvellous Méliès (o) for its assessment of Méliès' singular artistic personality.

Special gratitude is due to Professor Edwin Dawes for pinpointing the Maskelyne and Cooke repertory which Méliès saw in 1884. Every Méliès student owes a permanent debt to Madeleine Malthête-Méliès for her lifetime dedication to recovering and revealing the once-lost work of her grandfather.

Numbers in brackets refer to the notes at the end of the text; letters in brackets to works in the bibliography.

Illustrations come from British Film Institute Stills, Posters and Designs, the Cinémathèque Française and the private collections of Madame Madeleine Malthête-Méliès, Maurice Bessy, G.M. Lo Duca, Paul Hammond, Laurent Mannoni, Professor Edwin Dawes and the author.

CONTENTS

CELEBRATING THE MOVING IMAGE

The British Film Institute exists to encourage the development of film, television and video in the United Kingdom and to promote knowledge, understanding and enjoyment of the culture of the moving image. Its activities include The National Film Archive; The National Film Theatre; The London Film Festival; The Museum of the Moving Image; the production and distribution of film and video; Library and information services; Stills, Posters and Designs; Research; Publishing and Education; and the monthly Sight and Sound magazine.

The Museum of the Moving Image (MOMI) is a division of the British Film Institute.

DIRECTOR Wilf Stevenson
CONTROLLER BFI SOUTH BANK Jürgen Berger
CURATOR MOMI Leslie Hardcastle, OBE

DOSSIER DESIGN AND CONTENT
DESIGN Thumb Design Partnership
PRINTER The KPC Group
CONTENT David Robinson
DOSSIER MANAGEMENT Leslie Hardcastle, OBE
PICTURE RESEARCH Irene Long

COVER PHOTOGRAPH Eclipse de Soleil en Pleine Lune, 1907
INSIDE FRONT COVER PHOTOGRAPH Voyage dans la Lune, 1902
INSIDE BACK COVER PHOTOGRAPH Georges Méliès

Special thanks to Madame Malthête-Méliès for her support and encouragement in respect of this dossier and the Méliès Father of Film Fantasy Exhibition MOMI February 1993 – June 1993.

© Museum of the Moving Image, 1993
ISBN 0-85170-415-8

Museum of the Moving Image,
South Bank, Waterloo, London SE1 8XT

FROM MAGIC TO MOVIES

Nothing in the patrimony of Georges Méliès suggested that he would become an artist who would have the rare fortune to create his own unique art form. His natural destiny seemed rather to follow his father, a footwear tycoon, into the family business. The most colourful episode in the life of that father, Jean-Stanislas-Louis Méliès (1815-1898), born in Lavelanet (Ariege), was his apprenticeship in a kind of masonic order of shoe-makers. The rules of the order required the young man to travel the countryside – le Tour de France – practising his craft: he was given the name of "Carcassonne: l'Ami de Courage". On his return to Paris he met and, in 1843, married a young Dutch woman, Johannah-Catherine Schuering (1818-1899) who worked in the same factory. Catherine had grown up in the trade: her father was court bootmaker in the Hague until his workshops were burnt down during political turmoils in 1830, after which he emigrated with his family to France.

The young couple were ambitious, and in 1847 Louis Méliès set up his own workshop. By the time Georges Méliès was born on December 8 1861 Louis was a rich man, with his own factory, and a substantial country property.

Georges was much younger than his brothers Henri (born 1844) and Gaston (1852-1915) and by all accounts was very much indulged as a mother's boy. At seven he was enrolled in the Lycée du Prince Imperial, at Vanves. When the region was bombarded by the Prussians in 1870, the school was evacuated to Paris and the Lycée Louis-le-Grand. Méliès already had the passion for drawing which drove him for the rest of his life. People who watched him at work say that he would begin at one corner and gradually cover the paper with his elaborately detailed sketches, as if he were filling in a pre-existing outline. As a boy, too, he loved constructing toy theatres and marionettes.

Despite such extra-curricular distractions, he passed his baccalauréat in July 1880. It was assumed throughout the family that he would follow his brothers into the boot business; and moreover, that since Henri and Gaston had married two sisters, Georges would in the natural course of things marry the third and youngest of the siblings, who still remained available.

Such decisions were postponed however when Georges was called to do his military service, in the 113rd Regiment of Infantry. He served for one year and was discharged on November 12 1882 with the rank of corporal. His army records describe him as 1 metre 72 in height, blonde, with blue eyes.

Back in civilian life, Georges pleaded in vain to be allowed to attend the Ecole des Beaux Arts. His father, determined to save his son from a life of inevitable penury as a painter, insisted that he work in the factory. His first job was book-keeping under the stern eye of his mother. Working with the factory machinery proved more to his taste and he was able to introduce some ingenious modifications to the manufacturing process.

Caricature of Georges Méliès by Méliès

After two tedious years – still under threat of marriage to sister number three – came the escape which was to prove the turning point of his life. Early in 1884 Méliès was sent to London for a year to learn English. Perhaps too it was planned that he would eventually run the London office which the burgeoning enterprise shortly afterwards opened at 137 Cheapside, with a Mr T.G.Quickenden as their agent. (The London establishment later moved to Imperial Mansions, 178 Charing Cross Road).

Méliès' granddaughter recalls that he told her he lodged with a kindly lady called Mrs Atkins in Old Compton Street. Although the street directories of the period reveal no such name, it is quite possible that Mrs Atkins herself rented premises over one of the shops that filled the street. (The only London lodging house keepers of the name recorded in 1884 were Mrs Eliza Atkins at Gilbert Street, Grosvenor Square and Mrs Mary Ann Atkins at 2 Duke Street, Portland Place).

Méliès worked first for a boot and shoe shop which he remembered as "Mr Dobb". This is most likely to have been Robert Dobbie of 25 Jermyn Street and 198 Piccadilly: with the Méliès business connexions, Georges is likely to have had introductions to West End establishments. Similarly the clothing outfitter, "Mr Jones", for whom he subsequently worked was probably Jones and Co of 6 Regent Street (1).

To pass the evenings during his stay in London Méliès sought out those theatrical entertainments which placed the least strain on his small command of English.

If, as his granddaughter believes, he arrived in London in January 1884 he would have been in time to catch the end of the pantomime season. The repertoire that year uncannily anticipates his own future films. At Drury Lane there was *Cinderella*, which for one novelty scene dressed the chorus as fox-hunters, in pink satin cutaway coats, buckskin breeches, and top-boots – "a decided novelty" sniffed one critic, "though all persons may not admire its taste". An illustration of Mdlle Aenea, as the fairy Electra who flew down bearing the glass slippers, looks remarkably like one of Méliès' own etherial spirits. *Red Riding Hood* at Her Majesty's included a scene in which "one person is transformed into a wolf, another into a fox, and a third into an ape, by the stroke of the enchanter's wand"; though the critic felt that "the making of the wonderful rabbit-pie, and boiling the old lady in her own scullery copper, are somewhat too much prolonged". At the Alhambra, *The Golden Ring* included the perilous sea journey to the Isle of Storms. This was Méliès' world.

L'Armoire des frères Davenport, 1902

More significant however was his discovery of Maskelyne and Cooke, "Royal Illusionists", at the Egyptian Hall, Piccadilly. John Henry Maskelyne, a watchmaker, and his friend George Alfred Cooke, a cabinet maker, made their debut as illusionists in 1865 when they set out to expose the fakery of the Davenport Brothers, currently celebrated as "American spiritualist mediums". The Davenports' performance consisted of being tied and shut up in a cabinet. When the hall was put into complete darkness, a collection of musical instruments placed in the cabinet with them would begin to play and fly about. Maskelyne and Cooke reproduced the performance in full light, to prove that it was merely an illusion. Their Davenport Cabinet performance remained a favourite feature of their repertory, and Méliès himself would in time produce it both on stage and film.

The Davenport Brothers in their Cabinet, 1865

After extensive tours and a private show for the Prince of Wales, which led them to adopt the title "The Royal Illusionists and Anti-Spiritualists", Maskelyne and Cooke performed continuously at the Egyptian Hall, where Méliès discovered them, from 1873 until 1904 and the demolition of the building. Maskelyne and Cooke's most significant innovation was to incorporate their magical illusions into humorous or dramatic sketches – such as *Will, The Witch and the Watch*, built around the Davenport cabinet effect. Notable magicians who appeared in their shows included the French conjuror Bualtier De Kolta, whose sensational "Vanishing Lady" inspired one of Méliès' earliest trick films.

Publicity for Maskelyne and Cooke at the Egyptian Hall

The programme for Christmas 1883 which continued until February included the Davenport Cabinet Séance, Mr Maskelyne's "Thought Reading by Mechanism" and *Mrs Daffodil Downy's Light and Dark Séance*. In this an empty cabinet, standing on legs and free from all contact, was assembled in full view of the audience. Out of apertures in the cabinet

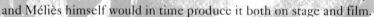

appeared a hand and arm; a violin played; a spirit form ("the Piccadilly Ghost") floated in the air; and finally an animated and illuminated skeleton pranced around, its skull and limbs becoming detached. After closure for alterations, the Egyptian Hall reopened in April with a new attraction, the famous automaton Psycho, who could do complex mathematical calculations and pick out playing cards. In July the summer programme introduced *Elixir Vitae, or Screvins in Two Pieces* involving the decapitation of a Gloucestershire farmer (Cooke) by Dr Bolus (Maskelyne). A new programme in September introduced Zoe, the sketching automaton.

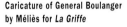

Caricature of General Boulanger by Méliès for *La Griffe*

Méliès may not have stayed on long enough for the Christmas programme, with *The Fakirs of Benares and their Brazen Oracle*, which included a decapitated head in a box, and anticipated Méliès' own delight in exotic settings for his magic.

In his "Mémoires", written in the third person, Méliès recalls, "This assiduous attendance made him, in a short time, a great amateur of the magic art. He studied this new theatrical style which was to augment his artistic baggage, and in two or three years, he himself became very skilful in the art of illusion. Returning to Paris, he was a frequent spectator of the Theatre of Illusions, created by the great thaumaturge Robert-Houdin, perfected himself and began to give performances, at first in drawing rooms, then at the Musée Grévin and the Galerie Vivienne"(c).

Méliès was increasing his "artistic baggage" in other ways. He developed his acting skills by performing dramatic monologues. For a brief period in 1889 he became a political cartoonist, contributing, under the name "Geo. Smile" to *La Griffe*, directed by his cousin Adolphe Méliès. The particular *bête noir* both of the magazine and its caricaturist was General Boulanger, whose political ambitions at that time threatened to overthrow the Republic.

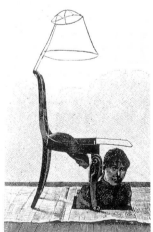

The Disappearing Lady on the Stage from Hopkins' *Magic*

Soon after his return from London, he met and married Eugénie Genin, the illegitimate daughter of a rich industrialist. Evidently the formidable Catherine Méliès was reconciled to abandoning her earlier matrimonial plans for Georges by the considerable dowry (said to be 50,000F) which Eugénie had inherited from her father. The young couple moved into an apartment on the fifth floor of the building at 5, rue Taylor, which housed both the family and its business.

In 1888 Louis Méliès decided to retire. His elder sons took over the footwear business; Méliès sold out his share. Now a man of substance, he did not hesitate when the chance came to buy the most famous magic theatre in Paris – if not the entire world – the Théâtre Robert-Houdin.

Robert-Houdin (1805-1871), who gave the theatre its name, is generally recognised as the father of modern conjuring. Opening his first theatre in the Palais-Royal in 1845, his distinction was the elegance, simplicity and style of his presentation. "I intended to have an elegant and simple stage, unencumbered by all the paraphernalia of the ordinary conjuror, which looks more like a toyshop than a serious performance . . . Of course I abstained from any eccentric costume, and I never thought of making any change in the attire civilized society has agreed to accept for evening dress, for I was always of the opinion that bizarre accoutrements, on the contrary, cast disfavour upon him" (2). (However extravagant the costumes Georges Méliès would adopt in films, on stage his habitual neat jacket, breeches, stockings and buckled shoes conformed to Robert-Houdin's precepts).

In 1853 or 1854 the lease on the Palais-Royal premises ran out, and a new theatre was constructed on the first floor of 8 Boulevard des Italiens. The small elegant room seated less than 200 persons; the stage was designed to look like an elegant Second Empire drawing room, though the simple furnishings concealed a mass of trapdoors and electrical equipment. Oddly, none of Méliès' biographers has noted

THÉATRE ROBERT-HOUDIN

8, Boulevard des Italiens

M. MÉLIÈS
Directeur

M. LEGRIS
Prestidigitateur

DU THÉÂTRE ROBERT-HOUDIN

Grandes Matinées de Prestidigitation

Tous les Jours Grandes Soirées Fantastiques

ABOVE: Seating arrangements at the Théâtre Robert-Houdin

LEFT: Programme for the Théâtre Robert-Houdin

that Robert-Houdin himself never appeared here. Before the move he had retired and handed on the show to his successor Hamilton (P.E.Chocat). After Robert-Houdin's death the lease and goodwill passed to his son Emile, whose widow sold it, for 40,000 F, to Méliès.

Méliès reopened the Théâtre Robert-Houdin in October 1888. At first attendances appear to have been poor, though they began to improve after December, when Méliès presented his first important original illusion, *La Stroubaika Persane*. In the course of the next seven years he was to create a score of illusions, generally sketches in the Maskelyne and Cooke style, but marked by Méliès' very personal style of comedy – generally they were described as "Scènes Burlesque". For instance in *Le Décapité récalcitrante* (1891), a clever illusion involving decapitation and a talking disembodied head was made more piquant by making the victim an incorrigibly boring lecturer whose flow of verbiage not even such extreme measures could stem. Other sketches – some of which were to be later reworked as films – included *L'Enchanteur Alcofrisbas* (1889), *Le Manoir du Diable* (1890), *Le Nain jaune* (1890), *Les Farces de la Lune ou Les Mésaventures de Nostradamus* (1891), *L'Auberge du Diable* (1894) and *Le Château de Mesmer* (1894). For all of these Méliès was inventor, designer, producer, mechanic and often performer, though he was supported on stage by the illusionists Harmington, Raynaly and, from 1894, Legris.

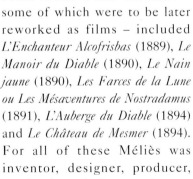

Caricature of Georges Méliès by Méliès

Drawing of the stage of the Théâtre Robert-Houdin after restoration, 1901

No less significant to Méliès' subsequent career as a film maker were the magic lantern projections which featured in his programmes. "For several years, and long before there was any question of animated pictures", he recalled, "the shows of the Théâtre Robert-Houdin

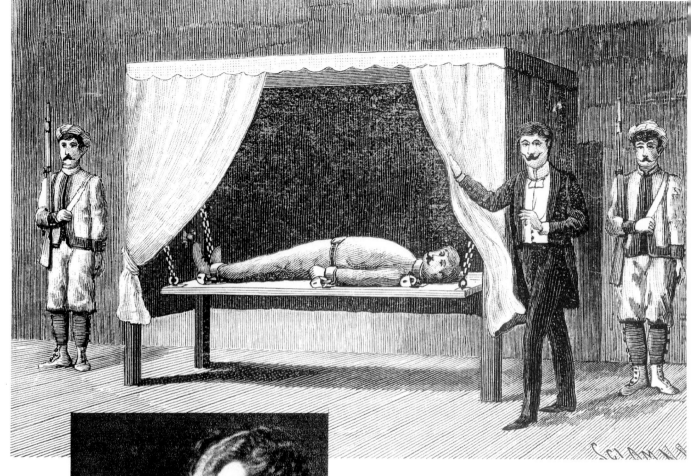

regularly ended with the projection of a series of coloured photographic views on glass (generally travel subjects accompanied by some hand-painted comic scenes, and chromatropes or kaleidoscopic slides, multicoloured, revolving and very pretty in effect). These projections were made with oxy-hydrogen lamps and with the aid of several Molteni lanterns, combined so that they permitted dissolving from one image to another. The system was analogous to the present-day

ABOVE: La Stroubaika Persane, Méliès' first important stage illusion, 1888

LEFT: Georges Méliès, the young magician

10

'dissolve' in moving pictures. Moreover different mechanical slides permitted different effects, such as: falling snow, lights, effects of day and night, vehicles moving along a road, railway trains, boats on a river etc. This was all done with slides that moved horizontally. This was in fact

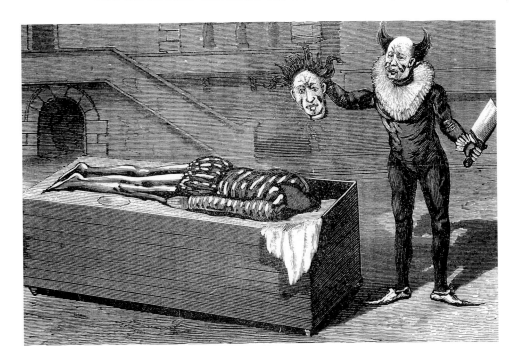

Decapitation explained, from Hopkins' *Magic*

the old magic lantern perfected, the precursor of the cinema. But the painted figures were immobile, unlike those of the cinema, and moved simply like the cut-outs of Ombres Chinoises. Despite these imperfections, the public liked these projections, because they were able to see unknown places and countries, remarkably photographed and prettily coloured. We recall this because we see that, long before the cinema, Méliès was very familiar with projections properly so-called, executed either with oxy-hydrogen or oxy-ether illuminants or with electric arc lights. From this point of view his education had

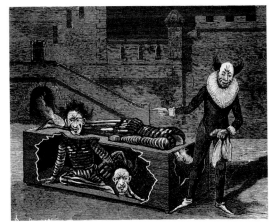

already been effected when he embarked on the cinema, and this was a distinct advantage for him, the illumination of cinematograph equipment being exactly the same, at least at that time" (c).

Méliès then was ready for the cinema.

THE ENCHANTED CINEMA

The first public show of the Lumière Cinématographe took place on the evening of December 28th 1895, in the basement of the Grand Café, 14 Boulevard des Capucines. In the afternoon there appears to have been a 'generale' – a special dress rehearsal for the press and other invitees – and there seems little doubt that Méliès was one of the audience at this performance. It would have been natural to invite him, since his theatre was the kind of venue in which the Lumières might have anticipated exploiting the Cinématographe. Moreover he was a near neighbour: the Théâtre Robert-Houdin was barely three minutes' walk along the Boulevards from the Grand Café. Intriguingly, less than three months earlier, Antoine Lumière, father of the brothers Auguste and Louis, had rented a large photographic studio directly over the Théâtre Robert-Houdin. If, as seems probable, his original plan had been to use these premises for the first showings of the Cinématographe, he would certainly have been in close contact with Méliès – who for his part might well have been less than enthusiastic about the installation of a rival attraction in the same building.

Interior of the Théâtre Robert-Houdin

The exact programme of this first demonstration of the Cinématographe is uncertain: in the course of 1895 the Lumières had shot some sixty films (each of 17m. or approximately one minute's running time); and programmes, generally consisting of ten titles, were variable. In the New Year however they were advertising a definite programme which included two of their earliest films, showing workers leaving the Lumière factory in Lyon and the delegates to a photographic congress in Lyon disembarking from a pleasure boat; genre subjects including blacksmiths, a child fishing goldfish out of a bowl, and a boat on a rough sea; and the first film comedy, *L'Arroseur Arrosé (Watering the Gardener)*(3). Whatever the films he saw, Méliès was greatly impressed and instantly saw the new invention as an ideal attraction for his theatre. He approached Antoine Lumière who was in charge of the show (Auguste and Louis had remained in Lyon). "At the end of the show, I made an offer to M.Lumière to buy his machine for my theatre. He refused. I even went up to 10,000F a sum which semed to me enormous. M.Thomas [director of the Musée Grévin], with the same idea, offered 20,000F without any better success. M.Lallemand, director of the Folies-Bergère, went to 50,000F. Wasted effort . . . M.Lumière remained adamant and replied to us amiably, 'This machine is a great secret and I do not wish to sell it. I want to exploit it exclusively myself"(4).

Méliès was not to be frustrated. Within three months he learned that Robert W.Paul, an instrument maker in Hatton Garden, London, was marketing a projector which used Edison Kinetoscope films, the Theatrograph (5). Méliès hurried to buy one and by April 4 he was able to project Edison films as part of the Robert-Houdin shows. Studying the Paul projector, Méliès set out to build a camera, with the help of two engineers, Korsten and Reulos. The work seems to have been carried out in the little workshop attached to the theatre, where conjuring apparatus and automata were made. Méliès claimed to have completed his camera in February, but a later date is more likely. By April at the latest however he appears to have had the apparatus in use. The first camera was large and enormously heavy, which limited portability but ensured the stability which was to prove essential for trick photography. It had no view finder, so the cameraman had to set up and focus each shot by means of a piece of ground glass or frosted celluloid placed in the open gate – the same technique used for ordinary plate cameras at the time. Like the still photographer, the early movie cameraman had to perform this operation under the shade of a black cloth.

Subsequently Méliès and his collaborators developed a more convenient apparatus, the Kinétographe, which was patented on 2 September 1896 by Méliès, Korsten and Reulos, and marketed commercially(6). As more production-line cameras came onto the market however Méliès abandoned the manufacture to Reulos, and for his own studio work adopted in turn cameras supplied by Gaumont, Demeny, Lumière and Pathé.

As Méliès recalled in his memoirs, the task of the first pioneers was "a real calvary". Everything had to be created or invented; and every inventor and pioneer jealously guarded the secrets of what he had himself discovered.

Having made his camera, film stock was the next problem. Méliès travelled to London, but found that Paul was unwilling to supply him with a small quantity – 20 17m. rolls – for experiment. He was thus obliged to buy a 45,000F stock of Eastman film – only to find when he opened it up back in Paris that it was not perforated. He commissioned a perforating machine from an engineer called Lapipe, but this proved "a veritable sledge-hammer"

Cylindrical supports for drying continuous film

which made only two holes at a time and required so much effort that, Méliès said, he was exhausted after a quarter of an hour.

Finally he had to devise his own equipment for developing and printing. At first, like other early film makers, he was obliged to cut up each film, develop it in pieces and then stick it together again when it was dry. The ingenious Méliès soon devised cylindrical supports to hold the continuous film and eventually built an electrically operated system of developing drums which he used for the rest of his film making career.

Méliès had also to discover and solve for the first time the problems of grading. Shot by daylight, his films were constantly subject to change of illumination, which required correction in the printing. Each member of his printing staff worked with a metronome and a chart showing the speed of exposure required for each section of film. With this guidance, the rate at which the handle of the printer was turned, and the intensity of the light source were constantly and appropriately varied.

By May or thereabouts Méliès was finally equipped to embark on production. His first one-minute film seems to have been *Une Partie de Cartes*, showing Méliès and two friends playing cards in his garden at Montreuil. The film has a special curiosity: Méliès in fact never played cards, because he said no-one would ever trust a prestidigitator at the table. The subject was directly imitated from Lumière, as were such titles as *L'Arroseur*, *Les Forgerons* and *Arrivée d'un Train*. Like his fellow pioneers Méliès at first filmed the kind of subjects an ordinary photographer with a still camera might have chosen. Most of the films were made in his gardens at Montreuil, though Méliès also transported his camera to Paris to photograph street views within easy reach of his theatre – La Place de l'Opéra and Boulevard des Italiens. Later in the year the photographic expeditions became more ambitious, as the camera was taken to the Bois de Boulogne and the Gare St Lazare, and to film bateaux-mouches on the Seine. In October Méliès covered the visit of the Tsar of Russia to Paris.

In July 1896 Méliès, taking his summer holiday, transported his massive camera,

Drawing for a piece of magical apparatus

Magic Cabinet for Le Nain Jaune

weighing 35 kilos, to Trouville and Le Havre, where he filmed a series of maritime views. He left a vivid account of the difficulties. In order to change the film he had to carry the camera, along with the rest of his equipment, to a chemist's shop – a laborious process which he did twenty times in the day. The wind blew away his black cloth, but "he was sustained by faith . . . and his views turned out well! How could he have

not been happy as a king?"(c). He was delighted with the results; the scenes of the stormy sea "fascinated the audience, used to the uniform representation of the sea in the theatre . . . What thrilled the public was to see for the first time a rigorously exact reproduction of nature. Those who were familiar with the sea cried, 'Oh it is just like that . . .!' and those who had never seen it imagined they were truly there"(c). This group of films also includes one of the rare instances in his career when Méliès used a moving camera. For *Panorama du Havre, pris d'un bateau* he placed his camera in a moving boat – a procedure which had already been employed by a Lumière cameraman, Promio, to film a panorama of the Grand Canal in Venice.

One of Méliès' earliest films showed him performing some tricks of prestidigitation in his garden. He was however quick to perceive that the

The magician Leglis and a butterfly lady on the stage of the Théâtre Robert-Houdin

Cinématographe provided a device for performing tricks undreamed of on the stage. Almost immediately he discovered the comic effects that could be produced by cranking the camera slowly so that the action was speeded up when the film was projected on screen. The titles *Dessinateur Express*, *Dessinateur: Chamberlain* and *Dessinateur: Reine Victoria* were almost certainly examples of speeded-up motion, as was *Dix Chapeaux en soixante secondes*.

Méliès' first true magic film however was *Escamotage d'une Dame chez Robert-Houdin*, made at the end of 1896. The vanishing lady illusion first performed by the Franco-Hungarian magician, Bualtier de Kolta (who had appeared at the Théâtre Robert-Houdin) was one of the most celebrated of all 19th century conjuring tricks. The lady was seated in a chair, which was placed on an open newspaper to prove that there was no communication with a trapdoor, and covered with a light silk cloth.

Escamotage d'une Dame chez Robert-Houdin, 1896

When the cloth was removed, the chair was empty. The lady then made her appearance from the wings. There was, of course, a trap-door, despite the newspaper and the illusion was accomplished by complicated machinery. Méliès himself had performed the trick on stage, but now realised that with the motion picture camera he could achieve the same result much more effectively and simply. All he had to do was to film the lady in the chair, stop the camera, remove the lady and then restart the camera.

In fact, this basic trick of stop-action, which represented the start and the basis of all Méliès' astonishing work with trick films, did not originate with him: more than a year earlier the device had been used for an Edison Kinetoscope film, *The Execution of Mary Queen of Scots*(7). Nevertheless Méliès undoubtedly found out the device for himself, and was the first European filmmaker to do so. Moreover he explored its artistic possibilities as no one else ever did. As his grandson Jacques Malthête-Méliès has recently written, "Even if Georges Méliès did not invent all the cinema tricks with which his work abounds, the fact is that he used them marvellously and magisterially" (y).

The story of the discovery has been retailed many times, and sounds almost too pat and colourful to be true. However, since Méliès set it down in 1907, long before the later years of nostalgia and mythmaking, we should perhaps give it some credit: "Would you like to know how I first had the idea of applying tricks to the cinématographe? Quite simply, I promise. The camera I was using in the beginning (a rudimentary affair in which the film would tear or would often refuse to move) produced an unexpected effect one day when I was photographing very prosaically the Place de l'Opéra. It took a minute to release the film and get the camera going again. During this minute the people, buses, vehicles had of course moved. Projecting the film, having joined the break, I suddenly saw a Madeleine-Bastille omnibus changed into a hearse and men into women. The trick of substitution, called the trick of stop action, was discovered, and two days later I made the first metamorphoses of men into women and the first sudden disappearances which, at first, had a big success. It is thanks to this very simple trick that I made the first *féeries: Le Manoir du Diable, Le Diable au Couvent, Cendrillon* etc." (a)(8).

Le Diable au Couvent, 1899

By 1898 Méliès was using stop-action effects regularly and enthusiastically, particularly for the films intended for use in the repertory of the Théâtre Robert-Houdin. In *Illusions Fantasmagorique ou La Boîte Mysterieuse* he used the effect at least half a dozen times in the course of one minute. Jacques Malthête-Méliès (y) has pointed out that these stop-action tricks required the negative to be cut and joined at each effect, since the speed of the camera varied on stopping and starting, necessitating the removal of a few frames at each join.

"One trick leads to another", wrote Méliès; "In face of the success of this new style, I set myself to discover new processes, and in succession I conceived dissolves from scene to scene, effected by a special arrangement in the camera; apparitions, disappearances, metamorphoses obtained by superimpositions on black backgrounds, or portions of the screen reserved in the décors; then superimpositions on white backgrounds already exposed (which everyone said was impossible before seeing them) which are obtained by a device which I am not going to reveal, since imitators have not yet penetrated the whole secret. Then came the tricks of decapitation, of doubling of characters, of scenes played by a single actor who, in multiplying himself, ends by representing as many as ten people, who play comedy among themselves. Finally, in employing the special knowledge of illusions which twenty-five years in the Théâtre Robert-Houdin had given me, I introduced into the cinema the tricks of machinery, mechanics, optics, prestidigitation, etc. With all these processes mixed one with another and used with competence, I do not hesitate to say that in cinematography it is today possible to realise the most impossible and the most improbable things" (a).

No doubt Méliès was inspired in his progressive discovery of new tricks for the camera by a book which was published in New York in 1897, *Magic – Stage Illusions and Scientific Diversions* by Albert A.Hopkins, editor of *The Scientific American*. Méliès would certainly have been one of the first purchasers of this monumental magic manual, not least since an appendix included his first major stage illusion *La Stroubaika Persane* – though it credited the original presentation to two German magicians, Lutz and Markgraf. The book included sections on Mysterious Disappearances, Optical Tricks, Ancient and Exotic Magic, Stage Effects and Automata, with an entire chapter on the projection of moving pictures.

We can certainly assume that Méliès studied with particular interest the chapter on "Trick Photography" which describes the techniques of 'spirit photography', superimposition on black backgrounds and reserves, duplex photography and methods of photographing disembodied heads.

Méliès first made use of 'spirit photography', achieved by simple double exposure, in *La Caverne Maudite and Rêve d'Artiste* (late 1898). His next film but one after these (according to the catalogue listing) was his first essay in multiple exposure on a black reserve. Normal double exposure produces an impression of combined transparent images; but if the second and subsequent images are superimposed over a black area on the frame, they appear solid. As Hopkins explained it, "In brief, the process consists in limiting the field of an objective so as to preserve intact for subsequent exposures the unused portion of the sensitised plate, and to be able to obtain upon the latter such combinations as may be desired of any number whatever of successive poses". Méliès simply substituted "film" for "sensitised plate". Sadoul describes the technique of *L'Homme de Têtes*:

"This number, presented as if performed on the stage of the Théâtre Robert-Houdin, uses black background, double exposure and masking. Behind the table, a reserve formed by a surface of black velvet provides a background against which, with the aid of three masks, Méliès three times superimposes his own head. To decapitate himself, he puts over his head a hood of black velvet so that against the black background the head becomes invisible. Stopping the camera permits the hood to be put on, and taken off to replace the head. The same stop allows the living head to be substituted for the cardboard head which Méliès has appeared to remove from his shoulders. The use of the black background ('black magic') avoids the 'impalpable spectres' of ordinary double exposure"(h).

Disembodied head illusion, Jehanne d'Alcy at the Théâtre Robert-Houdin

From this time Méliès used such photographic tricks with ever-growing skill and unabated enthusiasm. In 1899, for *Le Christ marchant sur les Eaux*, he superimposed a figure of Christ filmed in the studio upon a seascape which he had photographed during his holidays at Granville. Out of the double exposure developed the notion of the dissolve, a device used for the first time to link the tableaux in *Cendrillon* (1899). (It is worth noting however, that dissolves had been in use in magic lantern projections since the 1830s – a fact which Méliès himself acknowledges in his 1903 film *La Lanterne Magique*, where the images projected by the lantern are all dissolved one into another).

He was to use the black background technique for filmed conjuring tricks throughout most of his subsequent career; but two films remain masterpieces. In *L'Homme Orchestre* (1900), Méliès multiplies himself until he is seen as seven musicians all playing in unison. Twenty years later Buster Keaton repeated the effect, using precisely the same techniques in *The Playhouse*. (Keaton might very well have seen *L'Homme Orchestre* in the vaudeville theatres which he toured as a child; for his part Méliès was sardonic about the praise heaped on Keaton's "inventiveness").

Still more marvellous is *Le Mélomane* (1903), in which Méliès takes off his own head, six times, and throws the multiplying, grimacing heads onto telegraph wires, where they remain, to form musical notes. A chorus line marches on, and sings the music, which turns out to be "God Save the King". Jacques Malthête-Méliès rightly notes "The minutiae, the sum of work which these mere fifty metres of film necessitated, the production as confident as the montage, remain stupefying" (y).

Sketch of man with five heads for Le Mélomane, 1903

Another hint in Hopkins' *Magic* seems to have inspired Méliès early in 1902. Hopkins illustrates a whole series of photographs to show how the black background device can be used to create dwarfs and giants, and to produce effects of decapitated heads in wheelbarrows or on tables. In films like *Le Diable Géant* and *Nain et Géant* Méliès was able to improve upon Hopkins. Not only could he combine figures of different proportions, but by changing the distance between the actor and the camera he could make him seem to grow or shrink. The effect was completed by superimposing the growing or shrinking figure on to a scene with other figures of unchanging proportion. It should be noted that Méliès moved the figure before the camera, rather than moving the camera itself. This was because the success of camera trickery and superimpositions depended upon the absolute stability of the image, which a moving camera could not guarantee.

ABOVE: The head upon a plate from Hopkins' *Magic*

BELOW: Le Diable Géant, 1901

Méliès developed the idea further for his marvellous *L'Homme à la Tête de Caoutchouc*. The film shows Méliès in a laboratory. He places a duplicate of his own head on the table, and then sets about inflating it,

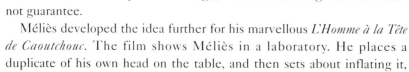

using a gigantic pair of bellows. His foolish assistant takes over, and energetically pumps so that the head grows and grows, grimacing and protesting all the time, until it finally bursts.

The effect was achieved by means of a little carriage, on which Méliès was moved towards the camera to produce the effect of the enlargement of the head. The disembodied head was then superimposed by double exposure upon the black reserve in the centre of the scene of Méliès' laboratory.

L'Homme Mouche (1902) introduced a trick which was to be frequently employed over the years – filming an actor in an inverted decor and then in turn inverting the image so that the actor appears to be walking on the ceiling. Again this must have been suggested by Hopkins' description of "Photographing a Catastrophe". By 1902 Méliès' repertoire of camera magic was more or less complete. For the rest of his career he would refine and develop his discoveries, always thinking up new and charming ways to put them to the service of fantasy.

Méliès' sketches and a frame from *L'Homme à la Tête de Caoutchouc*, 1902

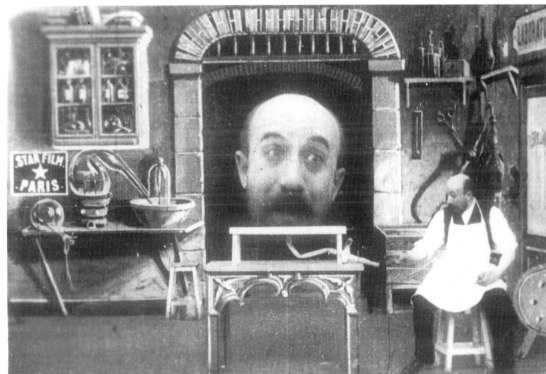

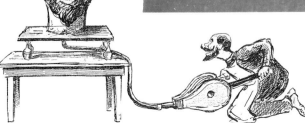

THE REVOLUTIONARY DISCOVERY: VUES COMPOSEES

Magic remained the central concern of Méliès' life and art. It was magic that first drew him to the cinema; magic that was his first contribution to the language of film. Throughout his career he was to continue to use the cinema to provide magical illusions for his theatre. Yet he himself often complained that his reputation as 'The Magician of Montreuil' and the world-wide love of his screen illusions overshadowed his other considerable contributions to the evolution and the repertory of the cinematographic art. For from the first Méliès proudly regarded cinema as art and himself as an artist.

In 1907 he perceptively summarized the historical development of the cinema up to that time: "At the beginning the views were exclusively subjects taken from life; later the cinematograph was employed as a scientific apparatus; finally it was to become a theatrical device. From the start, the first appearance of animated photography, the success was enormous, the result of curiosity; but when the cinematograph was put to the service of a theatrical art, that success was transformed into a triumph"(a).

If not alone, Méliès was certainly the most influential of those who effected this transformation and established the cinema as a narrative medium and theatrical spectacle. Today it is not easy to realise that for the inventors of the 1890s the achievement of making the image move was an end in itself. There was no obvious further use for the device. Auguste Lumière and his sons may truly have believed, in 1895, that it was a mere scientific curiosity without commercial future. The first one-minute films were no more than animated snapshots or picture postcards.

The picture on a postcard can, of course, tell a story, and there was already a rudimentary narrative in the Lumières' *L'Arroseur Arrosé*. The gardener is watering with a hose. A naughty boy creeps up behind and treads on the hose. The gardener peers into the nozzle to see why the water has stopped. The boy releases his foot and the gardener is drenched. The gardener chases the boy and spanks him.

This is the prototype of what Méliès called "vues composées" or "artificially arranged scenes". At first cinematographers filmed the world as it existed in front of their cameras. Méliès, before most others, was to demonstrate the possibility of arranging things in front of the camera, of organising and remaking the world that the cinematograph recorded. As always, there were precedents. For forty years the manufacturers of stereoscope views had staged scenes in their studios, with costumes and décors; and the production of photographic 'life model' lantern slides, even though the actors did not move, was very like the making of Méliès' "artificially arranged scenes".

Méliès arrived in the cinema, of course with what he called his "artistic baggage" – all the experience, the repertory, the costumes, décors and props of the Théâtre Robert-Houdin. Among his first films were shots of himself and other artists from his theatre – *Séance de Prestidigitation, Danse Serpentine, Miss De Vere (Gigue Anglaise), Le Papier Protée* – and 'scènes comiques'. By the end of 1896 he had erected a kind of bridge in his garden on which he could hang décors for illusions like *Escamotage d'une Dame chez Robert-Houdin* or *Le Manoir du Diable*. Clearly, though, the effect of back-drops gently rippling in the passing breeze was not long to satisfy a theatre professional like Méliès.

The building of a studio on the family property at Montreuil-sous-bois, near Paris seems to have been commenced around February 1897. Again, even if this was not the world's first studio (Edison's "Black Maria" preceded it by four years) Méliès created the basic model for film studios throughout most of the silent film period.

Building scenery at Méliès' Studio, c1904

The property stood at 74 bis, Boulevard de l'Hôtel-de-Ville, and was surrounded by a park of 8,000 square metres. In its original form the Montreuil studio was a large rectangular glass-house approximately 17 metres by 6 metres. At the southern end and at each side were large doors; and at the northern end was a scenery bridge framing the stage area, which ran the full width of the building. The stage area was at the same level as the rest of the floor. Behind the stage was a small artists' loge. The double-pitched roof rose from 4 metres at the sides to 6 metres at the apex. Sides and roof were glazed in frosted glass, except for an area of the roof which had clear glass to admit maximum light. A system of canvas blinds permitted regulation of the light intensity.

Around the end of 1899 the studio was enlarged and improved. The loge area behind the stage was extended, together with a second level – the ground floor providing the ladies' dressing room, the first floor the gentlemen's. Extensions were built at each side of the stage area to facilitate entry and exit, with doors so that cars and other vehicles could be driven across the scene. A recess was excavated beneath the stage, and the stage floor was equipped with a variety of trap-doors. Finally a small, corridor-like extension added in the middle of the south wall facing the stage provided accommodation for the camera when it was necessary to move it back for an exceptionally long shot – perhaps to create an image of an unusually diminished figure.

Other additions included a large tar-paper scenery hangar on the west side of the studio and a separate brick and concrete building on three floors, to house timber (on the ground floor) and the vast store of costumes, which Méliès claimed eventually numbered 20,000.

Méliès' innovations included the use of artificial lighting. In February 1897, about the time the studio was being built, he was commissioned to film the celebrated café-chantant artist Paulus performing a group of songs. Paulus apparently had an odd idea for exploiting the novelty of moving pictures by projecting these shots at the Ba-Ta-Clan café-concerts, while standing behind the screen, providing the voice. Only three of the five Paulus songs filmed on this occasion appeared in Méliès' catalogue: he pointedly omitted two in praise of his old aversion General Boulanger.

The Paulus films were shot inside the Théâtre Robert-Houdin by the light of 30 electric arcs – almost certainly the first successful use of artificial lighting in the history of the cinema. Méliès' subsequent attempts to use artificial light in the studio, where the stage area was much larger, were at first unsuccessful, though around the end of 1905 he installed an entire electrical lighting system. He boasted in 1907, "After many trials, and although the thing had been said to be impossible, I have recently succeeded, with a special electric installation . . . . in arranging artificial lighting which gives absolutely the result of daylight and which will in the future put in the shade the crude experiments of the past. Praise God! I shall not be driven mad . . . at least not by clouds . . . Diffused lighting is produced with the aid of a very large number of arc lamps and mercury vapour tubes combined. This artificial light is used together with daylight and makes it possible to vary the intensity at will"(a). The results may not however have been quite as satisfactory as Méliès claimed. In 1944 his widow recalled that the studio continued to depend on sunlight. "He tried with some neon tubes. He wasted 50,000F on that. The result was zero, it was too dark"(u).

Exterior Méliès' Studio

Not everything may have gone right: but for the next seventeen years the Montreuil studio was to be the sorcerer's workshop, the place where Méliès made a world of fantasy and enchantment.

Méliès' enterprise expanded rapidly in other directions. In 1896 he leased a shop at 14 Passage de l'Opéra, and subsequently took over nos 13, 16 and 17 also, to house his laboratory. In 1904 he installed a new laboratory in the studio at Montreuil. This enabled him to view his "rushes" immediately and to do any necessary retakes at once, rather than waiting a day while the film was taken into Paris for processing, by which time the cast might be dispersed and required to be called back at extra cost.

From the time of *Voyage dans la Lune* (1902) Méliès was increasingly angered by the unconscionable piracy of his work, particularly in the United States, where, says Charles Musser (*The Emergence of Cinema*, 1990), his pictures "had been duped by every American producer". Méliès tried various stratagems to defend himself. He began to place a small but prominent sign, showing the Star-Film trademark and the date of copyright, in every scene. For the sake of copyright, a paper positive of

Voyage dans la Lune, 1902

each film was deposited with the Library of Congress – where they still reside. He resolved to establish an office in New York (9), and in March 1903 sent his brother Gaston, who had retired from the footwear business after some financial misfortunes, to take charge of it. Gaston was joined by his son Paul, who later played in some American Méliès' productions. The office opened at 204 East 38th Street in June 1903, and a laboratory and factory were set up to produce prints from negatives shipped from Paris. This was much more economical than shipping multiple prints, each of which would have attracted import duties. To produce a second negative for America, Méliès henceforth consistently used two cameras. Gaston, as agent, received a salary plus 25 to 40 per cent of the profits, which for a time produced a very handsome income.

Méliès' Company Logo

The first American Star-Film catalogue fiercely attacked those American manufacturers who "found it easier and more economical fraudulently to copy the Star Films and to advertise their poor copies as their own original conceptions . . . In opening a factory and office in New York we are prepared and determined energetically to pursue all counterfeiters and pirates. We will not speak twice, we will act"(v).

However much his activities and his staff expanded, however, Méliès remained a one-man band – his self-multiplication in *L'Homme Orchestre* seems symbolic. Lucien Astaix, one of his cameramen, recalled many years later, "He was an individualist. A true artist, a lot of talent, an oddball do-it-yourselfer. He had a strong sense of cinema. He had the instinct of how to put together a script. We could never figure out what kind of film we were going to make. He had everything in his head, no written script. He used to put together the cast and crew, and we were shooting. He was preparing the story all by himself. Everything was ready. He was building the props and scenery by himself. He was also very good at using a hammer and pliers, but we could never find out what we were going to do . . ."(y).

Méliès himself has left an account of his normal, adrenalin-driven working day at the height of his career. He would get up at 6 and be at the studio by 7 to work on painting and constructing décors, and making accessories. Working under the glass roof which in summer could produce temperatures of 40 or 45 degrees, he continued until 5, when he travelled into Paris. From 6 to 7 he was at his office, receiving people and dealing with business. After a rapid dinner, he arrived at the Théâtre Robert-Houdin by 8, to supervise the performance. His only relaxation consisted of sketching during the moments when he was not occupied on the stage. After the show he would return to Montreuil and get to bed around half past midnight. During all this period, he said, he rarely slept more than six hours a night. Having spent Monday to Thursday in preparation,

Friday and Saturday were reserved for shooting the tableaux made ready during the week. These days, he said, were the worst in terms of fatigue, since he was at the same time producer, machinist and actor. On Sundays and holidays – "in order to rest" he said ironically – he had a matinee at the theatre from 2 to 5, three continuous performances of films from 5 to 7 and a further live performance from 8 to 11.30. Not surprisingly he attributed this staggering activity to his "great power of resistance to fatigue".

Each August, when the heat made the studio intolerable, Méliès and his family would spend the month by the sea. Inevitably Méliès passed the time devising and designing new illusions. On 15 August however he would regularly race up to Paris for the day, and spend three hours shooting a short film, "in order not to leave his clientele a month without some novelty".

Scene preparation at Méliès' Studio

A number of photographs showing Méliès at work have survived, and they seem to confirm his widow's memory that "he was always in good spirits. I never saw him angry on the set. It seems that he got extremely upset once, but I wasn't there. He was never impolite. He prepared his stuff, and then he said: 'you, you are going to do such and such'. When he realised that someone didn't listen, he didn't say anything special, he just warned him: 'Mr so-and-so, I told you this several times, I'm getting tired of it'. If it happened again, he suspended him for three weeks . . . He played the scene for them. He explained everything very much in detail. And when he realized that they were spending their time making jokes or pinching the girls, he said, 'Look, I'm working hard and you're just fooling around, so you can stay home next time' Afterwards if they complained, he would say, 'You want to have fun here, but I don't have time for that'".

Particularly for trick work and double exposures, he depended upon extreme precision from his performers: 'If you are making ten exposures and in one of them an actor makes an imprecise gesture, in which his arm passes in front of a character photographed in the next exposure, it results in transparencies and a dissolve effect that wrecks the trick". He did not minimise the problems: "Beyond that, think of the difficulty and anger that possesses you when, after three or four hours' work and minute attention, the film tears at the seventh or eighth superimposition and obliges you to abandon the whole thing and start again, since you cannot repair a torn film when it has a still latent image on it – it can only be developed once, after the tenth and last exposure has been made . . . "

"Apart from all these obstacles, that is the difficulties inherent in this kind of scene, the cinematographer has still more problems: variations in the light, clouds obscuring the sun, accidents to the camera, films jamming or tearing, insensitivity of the emulsion, spots on defective film which only appear after development and which make it unusable, little holes imperceptible to the eye transforming themselves into great rocks when projected. That's what makes it such a comfort when, after development, the take is perfect. No-one among the profane can ever know the degree of patience, perseverance and will necessary to succeed. I have to smile when I hear people say, 'How is it that these films cost so much?'"(a).

At first Méliès discovered – in common with most other early film makers – that professional actors felt it beneath them to work before the camera and for his early films he pressed his family, friends and staff into service. He complained though that these non-professionals appeared clumsy and uneasy in the period costumes which he favoured. Hence he began to attract the dancers from the Châtelet, who were happy to supplement their paltry pay. Soon they were followed by dancers from the Opéra. In turn came performers from the Parisian cafés-chantants. Even the English stars Little Tich and Harry Fragson – both celebrities of the French music halls – made guest appearances.

In time Méliès found himself turning away aspirants. He noted that the least adept were legitimate actors from the Comédie Française who, deprived of words, tended to compensate by over-acting. Nor were they equal to the degree of acrobatism which Méliès' films often demanded. In this line one of his happiest discoveries was the agile young André Deed, soon to become the cinema's first great international comedian.

In the trick films primarily designed for the Théâtre Robert-Houdin the performers – the lead was invariably Méliès himself – deliberately act to the camera, presenting their illusions directly to the audience exactly as they would on stage. For his dramatic films on the contrary Méliès had quite different, exacting and remarkably sophisticated principles of acting. "Cinematic mime demands a whole study and special qualities. The actor no longer has an audience to address, either in speech or mime. The only spectator is the camera, and nothing is worse than to look at it and to take notice of it when playing, which invariably happens the first time with actors used to the stage rather than the cinema. The actor must imagine that he has to make himself understood, whilst remaining silent, to deaf people who are watching him. His playing has to be quiet, very expressive; few gestures, but gestures that are clean and clear. Perfect

Deux cent mille lieues sous les mers ou Le Cauchemar d'un Pêcheur, 1906

COPYRIGHTED
BY GEO. MÉLIÈS 1906
PARIS NEW-YORK
Trade-Mark ★ Star

Voyage à travers l'Impossible,
1904

expressiveness of the face, very exact poses are indispensable. I have seen numerous scenes played by known actors who were not good because the principal element of their success, the word, became a positive disadvantage in the cinema. Used to talking, they employ gesture only as a subsidiary to the word in the theatre, while in the cinema, the word is nothing, gesture everything"(a).

Méliès was justly proud of his own performances and make-ups, playing "the most diverse personages and making himself unrecognisable with clever make-up"(c). His great-grandson calculates that he played some 320 different roles in his films over the years. In twenty films he played Mephistopheles, Beelzebub or Satan; and in at least one hundred more, the prestidigitator, magician or sorcerer.

Though the protean Méliès seems often to have operated the camera himself, his first official cameraman was one Leclerc. Leclerc had the misfortune to be caught by the police selling pornographic photographs, and was succeeded by Michaut, who in turn left to form a distribution company, American Kinematograph with two other ex-Méliès employees, Lallement and Astaix. Another cameraman, P. Tainguy ultimately went to the American branch.

**Méliès as Mephisto.
Programme for the Gala Méliès,
1929**

From the time Méliès began to work with two cameras, in order to make an American as well as a European negative, the second camera operator was frequently his young daughter Georgette Méliès, who also served when necessary as a projectionist. She seems also to have projected the advertising films which Méliès showed at night in the street outside the theatre. Georgette was no doubt the first woman in the world to perform either of these jobs.

THE MANY WORLDS OF GEORGES MELIES

In 1899, when Méliès made *L'Affaire Dreyfus* and his first *Cendrillon*, they were something new and revolutionary. At a time when the general run of films shown to the public were one-shot, one-incident, one-minute affairs, Méliès put together a whole succession of films, each a separate scene as in the theatre, to relate a continuous story lasting, in the case of the Dreyfus film, some 12 minutes. (Although *Cendrillon* was marketed as a single picture, with dissolves between the scenes, *L'Affaire Dreyfus* was sold as twelve separate one-minute films: whether the whole suite was shown together depended on the enterprise or audacity of the individual exhibitor).

When he made his last films – which included a new *Cendrillon*, at 30 minutes five times longer than the earlier one – his filmic method had hardly altered. The one-scene-one-shot tableau story-telling and fixed camera view seemed hopelessly antiquated to the audiences of 1912, accustomed to the fast, dynamic

Cendrillon, 1899

editing and constantly shifting viewpoints that D.W.Griffith had developed at Biograph.

Today we can appreciate better that this was the Méliès style. His art lay in mise-en-scène and mise-en-shot. For quite practical reasons the trick techniques which remained a feature of his work demanded a perfectly stable – and so immobile – camera. Méliès' whole aesthetic depended on a unity of viewpoint, "which is fixed at about 1 metre 30 above stage level, in the median axis of the scene and at a distance from the frame of the stage which permits the camera to take in the full width of that frame" (Jacques Malthête-Méliès). The two-dimensional décors were painted in trompe-l'oeil perspective (10) centred on this point of view. The Star-Film slogan was "Le monde a la portée de la main". The world – or worlds – in the grasp of Méliès' hand were created within this single viewpoint of his 6 metre wide stage. Telling his stories through the succession of tableaux scenes, he justly boasted that his narrative was so clear that sub-titles were never necessary in his films. This, he shrewdly observed "was (in the period of silent films) the perfect formula for the international cinema"(c).

Cendrillon, 1899

Yet within these limits, in the course of sixteen years and upwards of 500 films, Méliès explored practically every genre. "I must tell you", he wrote, "that contrary to the reputation which I have been given of being exclusively the king of tricks and fairy tales or the Jules Verne of the Cinema (because this is what I have been called), I have, on the contrary, from the beginning, attempted all genres: historical scenes, dramas, comedies, actualities, reconstitutions, operas and operas-comiques with reduced scores, publicity films, special films for the theatres (La Cigale, Châtelet, Folies-Bergère), war scenes, antique scenes, mythological scenes, etc. If I have brought all sorts of tricks to the cinema, I am proud above all of having launched the cinema upon the theatrical road, which has succeeded so well".

After the trick films, the *féeries* are perhaps Méliès' most characteristic work – those fast, light-hearted, irreverent retellings of nursery stories, peopled by comic grotesques and (most important) shapely dancing girls, played out in fantasy-baroque settings with jokes about motor cars and balloons and other anachronisms. The style had its origins in the theatre – in comic opera, in the English pantomimes and the ballets which Méliès had no doubt seen at the Alhambra and the Empire during his London sojourn, above all in the *féeries* properly called, performed at the Eden and Châtelet Theatres in Paris. The presentations in the Théâtre Robert-Houdin itself seem often to have been miniature versions of the big stage spectacles of these theatres. Méliès maintained links with the Châtelet throughout his film career, and recruited many of his actresses and dancers from the chorus. *Robinson Crusoe* (1902) was probably based on an 1899 Châtelet production of the same subject. *Le Royaume des Fées* (1903) was based on an old stage favourite, *La Biche aux Bois* by the Guignard Frères originally produced in 1845. A notable revival of this spectacle in 1897 had introduced a short film of pretty female sprites (filmed on 70mm film by Georges Demeny and hand coloured) into one scene.

For Christmas 1905 Méliès was commissioned to produce a film episode for the Châtelet's *Les quatre cents Farces du Diable*, a new version of an old *féerie*, *Les Pilules du Diable*, originally produced at the Cirque Olympique in 1839. The scene provided by Méliès showed an "astral carriage" passing through the heavens and ultimately tumbling down to

Les Aventures de Robinson Crusoe, 1902

earth. When the long run of the show ended on 10 June 1906, Méliès used the scene – one of his most inventive and beautiful creations – as the centrepiece for a filmic recreation of the Châtelet piece, retitled, so as not to risk any copyright problems, *Les quatre cents Farces du Diable*.

Among his other major *féeries* were *Cendrillon* (1899), *Rêve de Noël* (1900), *Le Petit Chaperon Rouge* (1901), *Barbe Bleue* (1901), *Le Palais des mille et une Nuits* (1905), *Jack le Ramoneur* (1906), which bore a striking resemblance to Kingsley's *The Water Babies*, *La Fée Carabosse ou Le Poignard Infernal* (1906), the second *Cendrillon* (1911) and *Les Aventures du Baron Munchausen* (1911).

LEFT: Rêve de Noël, 1900

BELOW & BELOW LEFT: Les quatre cents Farces du Diable, 1906

BOTTOM: Barbe Bleue, 1901

Often the *féeries* merge into the category of burlesques, in which Méliès included the irresistibly manic *Robert Macaire et Bertrand* (1906), and *Le Tunnel sous la Manche, ou Le Cauchemar Franco-Anglais* (1907), in which Méliès involved President Fallières and King Edward VII in some characteristic Star-Film adventures including train collisions, explosions and the Salvation Army.

Le Palais des mille et une
Nuits, 1905

An equally fine line divides the *féeries* and burlesques from the fantastic journeys and science fiction which sweetly tease the solemnity of Jules Verne and H.G.Wells' *The First Men in the Moon*. Like them Méliès transports us to far-off worlds – 20,000 leagues under the sea or into the atmosphere – but his worlds, however exotic the setting, the flora and the fauna, are still reassuringly crowded with music hall grotesques and pretty *Belle Epoque* chorus girls.

Méliès' most famous work remains *Voyage dans la Lune* (1902), which retains all its vitality and charm after more than ninety years. "The idea of *Voyage dans la lune* was given to me by Jules Verne's book *De la terre à la lune*. In this the men cannot reach the moon, go around it, and come back to earth, after having, in fact, failed in their expedition. So I imagined, using Jules Verne's procedure (cannon and shell), reaching the moon, so as to be able to compose a certain number of original and amusing *féerique* views of the interior and exterior of the moon, and to show some monsters, inhabitants of the moon, while adding one or two artistic effects (girls representing the stars, comets etc., snow effect, bottom of the sea, etc) . . .

Frame stills and sketches by Méliès, Voyage dans la Lune, 1902

"The film cost around 10,000F, a relatively large sum for the time, due principally to the mechanical machinery and mainly to the cost of costumes of cardboard and cloth made for the Selenites or inhabitants of the moon. Their shells, heads, feet, everything was made specially, and in consequence expensive. I myself made the models done in clay, and the plaster moulding and the costumes were made by a maker of special masks, used to working in papier mache . . . "

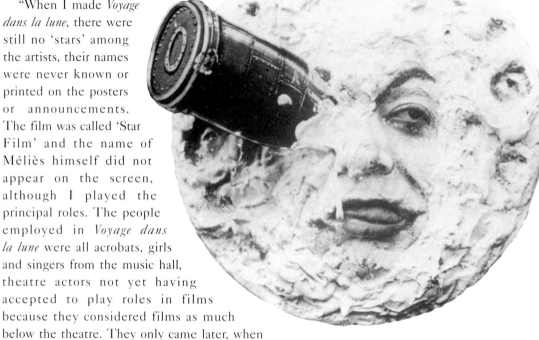

"When I made *Voyage dans la lune*, there were still no 'stars' among the artists, their names were never known or printed on the posters or announcements. The film was called 'Star Film' and the name of Méliès himself did not appear on the screen, although I played the principal roles. The people employed in *Voyage dans la lune* were all acrobats, girls and singers from the music hall, theatre actors not yet having accepted to play roles in films because they considered films as much below the theatre. They only came later, when they learned that the music hall people earned more money playing in films than they did working in the theatre, for some 300 francs a month . . . In the cinema they could earn double. Two years after this, my office was every evening full of theatre people wanting jobs."

"I remember that in *Voyage dans la lune* the moon (the lady in a crescent) was Bleinette Bernon, a music hall singer, the stars were ballet girls from the Châtelet, and the men (the principals), Victor André, from the Théâtre de Cluny, Delpierre, Farjaux, Kelm, Brunnet, music hall singers and myself. The Selenites were acrobats from the Folies-Bergère"(11).

ABOVE & LEFT: Voyage dans la Lune, 1902

Méliès may also have been in part inspired by a chapter in Hopkins' *Magic* which described a lantern entertainment, "A Trip to the Moon", though his personal fascination with the moon evidently pre-dated this. At the Théâtre Robert-Houdin he had presented *Les Farces de la Lune ou Les Mésaventures de Nostradamus* in July 1891; and in 1899 had made a film called *La Lune à un Mètre*.

ABOVE & BOTTOM LEFT: Voyage dans la Lune, 1902

ABOVE & BACKGROUND TO PAGE: Eclipse de Soleil en Pleine Lune, 1907

Méliès several times returned to the fantastic voyage formula for major productions: *Voyage à travers l'Impossible* (1904), *Le Raid New York-Paris en Automobile* (1908), *A La Conquête du Pôle* (1912) and *Deux cent mille lieues sous les mers, ou Le Cauchemar d'un Pêcheur* (1906), which multiplied by ten the depth of Jules Verne's original imaginary expedition. Perhaps Méliès' greatest success in this genre after *Voyage dans la Lune*, *Le Raid Paris-Monte-Carlo en deux heures* was specially commissioned by Victor de Cottens and the Isola Brothers for a 1904 revue at the Folies-Bergère, where it ran for 300 performances. Cottens himself appears, along with Little Tich and Harry Fragson, in the opening scene of the film, where King Leopold is seen off from the Place de l'Opéra.

Opera – along with Méliès' penchant for diabolical characters – inspired *Faust aux Enfers ou La Damnation de Faust* (1903), after Berlioz, and *Faust et Marguerite* (1904), after Gounod. *Faust et Marguerite* was the subject of rather extravagant advertising in the New York Star-Film catalogue, which boasted that "The personnel of the 500 characters depicted in this stupendous production were engaged from 19 different theatres in Paris, among whom were fifty dancers from the 'corps de ballet' of the Grand Opera House in Paris"(v).

Despite this undoubted exaggeration, these films were innovatory in that the catalogue announced that exhibitors might purchase specially arranged music for piano for $2.50. Indicating the prestige of the films, the catalogue also advises: "*The Damnation of Faust*, which we have already published, and which has met with considerable success, forms a

Voyage à travers l'Impossible, 1904

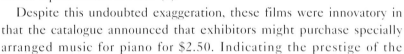

Le Raid Paris-Monte-Carlo en deux heures, released 1905

natural sequence to this marvellous and unprecedented work we are today presenting to the public . . . Several of our faithful patrons and friends have already decided to introduce these works in their programmes upon two successive nights. On the first *Faust and Marguerite* will be given, and on the second *The Damnation of Faust* thus bringing twice the public to view them through the intense interest arising from these subjects, which never fails for a single instant"(v).

The tragic theatre inspired an 8-minute *Hamlet, Prince de Danemark* (1907) and *Shakespeare: La Mort de Jules César* (1907). *La légende de Rip Van*

La Damnation de Faust, 1903

Winckle (1905) was from a comic opera of 1884, based on the story by Washington Irving. One of the earliest historical pieces was the 1900 *Jeanne d'Arc*, which the catalogue mendaciously advertised as boasting around 500 persons on the scene, in superb costumes (the number was certainly nearer fifty).

In the class of melodrama, Méliès included *Un Rêve de Noël* and *Les Incendiaires, ou L'Histoire d'un Crime* (1906). This realistic contemporary crime story fell foul of the censorship on account of a too convincing scene of the guillotine which ended the film, and which Méliès was obliged to remove.

A la Conquête du Pôle, 1912

Deux cent mille lieues sous les mers ou Le Cauchemar d'un Pêcheur, 1906

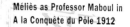

Méliès as Professor Maboul in A la Conquête du Pôle 1912

Exceptional in Méliès' work is the mordant irony of the curious *La Civilisation à travers les Ages* ("Tour à tour dramatique, pathétique, naturaliste, comique, satirique et ironique"), which ends its chronicle of centuries of inhumanity with "Le Triomphe du Congrès de la Paix" – a vision of a battlefield strewn with the dead and dying.

The 'fake' newsreels which were a feature of the early years of cinema are somewhat puzzling to us today, accustomed as we are to a total motion picture coverage of the world's events. To audiences of 1900 it was less surprising. Pictorial magazines regularly used artists' impressions rather than photographs to illustrate current events and dramatic recreation before the cameras was not so different. The economic basis of the cinema at that period was not such that anyone could dream of travelling to far-off places to film current happenings. Moreover civic and police authorities were generally intolerant of photographers in public places.

So it was that Méliès recreated in his studio the eruption of the volcano Mont Pelée in Martinique, a balloon catastrophe and the wreck of the battleship 'Maine' in Havana. In 1899, just after the second trial of Captain Dreyfus, Méliès made his reconstruction of *L'Affaire Dreyfus*. The sensational case, with its shocking undertones of anti-Semitism, had divided France for a number of years, caused the resignation of several ministers, the suicide of one of the principal witnesses Colonel Henry, and the trial of Emile Zola. The twelve tableaux of Méliès' film in large degree give the impression of a series of wax-work tableaux; yet it comes vividly to life with a scene in which the press reporters rush excitedly from the court of Rennes, giving a remarkable sense of actuality as they run towards and past the camera. The measure of the film's effect in its own day is that its first Paris showings provoked fights between partisans of the opposing sides and resulted in the film being banned by the Paris Prefecture.

Even more spectacular though was Méliès' staging of the coronation of King Edward VII. Since cameras were not allowed in Westminster Abbey, the Warwick Trading Company, who distributed Méliès' films in England, commissioned him to restage the ceremony. Charles Urban and George Albert Smith of Warwick sent him a dossier of pictorial reference

Les Incendiaires ou L'Histoire d'un Crime, 1906

material, and Méliès built the set – a much reduced interior of Westminster Abbey – in the garden at Montreuil, ordered the costumes and cast a waiter as the King and a dancer from the Châtelet as the Queen. More than half a century later George Albert Smith recalled that he and Urban went to Paris for the filming and that he himself operated the camera while Méliès directed the scene.

Méliès was chagrined that despite all the publicity surrounding the banning of cameras in the Abbey and the costly and elaborate staging of his production, one Paris journalist attacked him as a counterfeiter. Méliès replied with dignified irony that he had not been charged with counterfeiting when he filmed the life and death of Joan of Arc and Julius Caesar.

A remarkable footnote to Méliès' activity was his role as (apparently) the first producer of film commercials. Around 1900 he made a series of some fifteen advertising films: the products promoted included Delion hats, Mystère corsets, Falires phosphatine, Meunier chocolate, Bornibus mustard, Nestlé baby food (for which the actor was the infant André Méliès), and Veuve Bruno polish. These films were projected in the street outside the Théâtre Robert-Houdin.

ABOVE & FAR RIGHT: La Civilisation à travers les Ages

LEFT: Eruption Volcanique à la Martinique

THE END – AND AFTER

The greatest homage paid to Méliès by his peers during his active career can also be seen in hindsight as the beginning of his downfall. In 1909 he was elected President of the first Congrès International des Editeurs du Film, which took place in Paris between 2 and 4 February. The major film making countries – France, Britain, Italy, Germany, Russia and the United States – were represented; and a group photograph, taken at the end of the conference, after a banquet in honour of George Eastman, shows Méliès, cane and silk hat in hand, at the centre of a genial group of distinguished tycoons that included Pathé, Eastman and Gaumont.

Despite the apparent good humour of the photograph, the congress saw some hard debates. Méliès was proud to have succeeded with a motion to standardise perforation systems. There had been a fiercer battle over a proposal by Pathé to standardise film prices. Méliès, whose own films cost much more than those of most other producers, opposed this bitterly, and won the day, though not without some acid exchanges. According to Méliès' own account, Pathé sneered, "You, you will never be anything but an 'artist'. I am a business man. You will never be that, because you do not understand that if our business is to grow, what matters above all is to have a lot of clients, and for that we have to sell as cheaply as possible"(c).

Méliès recalled that he rose, very calm, and retorted quietly, "I am only an artist. Well, that is already something! But that is precisely the reason I do not agree with you. I say: the cinema is an Art, because it is the product of all the arts. Therefore, either the cinema will progress and perfect itself, to become more and more artistic, or, if it remains stationary and without possible progress, by restricting the

Méliès at the first Congrès International des Editeurs du Film, 1909

46

prices, it will quickly decline! That is the clear truth. As far as I am concerned, do not think that I feel myself insulted in being disdainfully called 'artist', because if you, the 'business man' (and nothing else, therefore incapable of producing composed views), have not artists to make them for you, I ask myself what will you sell?"(c).

One resolution however was to prove a decisive disaster for Méliès' business. The decision was taken henceforth to rent films, and abandon the old system of selling them outright. Méliès' organisation was not equipped for the huge complications of such a trade. Moreover rental demanded a liquid capital and he had consistently invested his capital to the hilt in his film making and facilities. The rental system was also rapidly to bring about the demise of the travelling fairground cinematograph showmen, who had formed an important section of Méliès' clientele.

The cinema industry had moved on too fast for Méliès. He belonged to the first generation of independent, artisan producers. The first decade of the new century had seen the rise of great capitalist enterprises, like Gaumont and Pathé, by 1909 the biggest producer in the world.

Méliès had resisted several earlier offers of distribution partnerships, notably from the Eclair company; but by 1910 he seems to have been distributing his films through Gaumont. By this time his output had become smaller and somewhat intermittent, and he was involving himself more with the theatre. In 1909 he produced an adaptation of a Robert-Houdin sketch, *Les Phénomènes de Spiritisme* at the Folies-Bergere and the following year mounted a spectacle, *Les Fantômes du Nil* at the Alhambra and Olympia in Paris and subsequently took the production on tour.

Towards the end of 1911, clearly experiencing financial difficulties, Méliès entered into an arrangement with Pathé, who was to finance and distribute Méliès' films on a profit sharing basis. Subsequently the production arrangement seems to have been revised: Pathé instead made a loan to Méliès against the security of the Montreuil studio.

Under this arrangement he made his six last films. In 1911 he created *Les Hallucinations de Baron Munchausen* and *Le Vitrail diabolique*; in 1912, *Cendrillon, ou La Pantoufle Mystérieuse* and two final fantasies, *A la Conquête du Pôle*, and *Le Chevalier des Neiges*. Méliès last film was an adaptation from a Labiche farce, *Le Voyage de la famille Bourrichon*.

According to the bitter testimony of Méliès' widow the films were brutally shortened and re-edited by Pathé's production chief, Ferdinand Zecca. In her eyes Zecca's butchery was the action of a jealous and (certainly) much less talented man. Yet – anticipating as it does so many subsequent studio horror-stories – the treatment of Méliès by the Pathé studios may well have indicated that he was already a man of the past.

With all their charm and skill, these films, with their tableaux structure, were anachronisms in an age which had experienced the speed, vitality and open spaces of Griffith's Biograph films, and was about to see *Cabiria* and *Birth of a Nation*.

Meanwhile Gaston Méliès' American enterprise had gone through its own evolution of rise and – at this inappropriate moment – decline.

Gaston Méliès began to film occasional actualities soon after setting up the office and factory in New York. On August 22 1903 he photographed a yacht race (*Reliance-Shamrock III*) and the film duly appeared in the Star-Film Catalogue. In 1905 the catalogue also added *Le Président elu Roosevelt, le vice-président Fairbanks et leur escorte se rendant au Capitole de Washington*, which must have been shot in February of that year. Later actualities included *The Catholic Centennial Celebration* (1908).

In October 1908 it was reported that Gaston had established a production company in Chicago, with a capital of $15,000, and studios at the Criterion Theatre. Gaston and Paul were named as technical directors, and Lincoln Carter was the director. Soon Gaston had acquired a license to turn out a reel a week for the Edison Trust. The following year the enterprise moved to Fort Lee, New Jersey, where the Pathé and Eclair companies had already established a Franco-American film colony.

In 1944 Paul Méliès recalled: "In 1910 my father Gaston Méliès sent me with a score of actors, a director and cameraman to the extreme south of Texas, to San Antonio, an old Spanish colonial town two hundred kilometres from the Mexican border. We organised a studio, a simple open-air stage surrounded by poles supporting wires on which were hung skins. We filmed by sunlight. It never rains in Texas".

"It was there we shot *The Immortal Alamo* and another big film about the war of Secession. The cameraman William Paley was American, the director a big Irishman with a red nose. In our troupe Francis Ford [John Ford's elder brother] played the heroic roles. I lived near San Antonio in a house called the Star Film Ranch, beside a river. There was nothing but cactus on the horizon. Every morning at 7 our cowboys arrived, took out their revolvers and started firing. Most of them were part Indian. They were very good looking people. We stayed there all winter, six months. When the summer came it was impossible. Then we came back. After that my father took over the production, with a Frenchman as director".

After 1911 the Gaston Méliès productions were called "American Wild West" and adopted the trademark of a horse's head in a horse shoe. In winter 1911, Gaston and Paul again left for San Antonio to resume western production, but Gaston found the country too rough and took the unit to California. There they eventually established themselves at Santa Paula, North of Los Angeles. Paul Méliès recalled: "He bought a house and built an open-air studio. He made westerns and war films, quite stupid but very successful. The story was always the same: a young man loved a girl, a villain carried her off, the young man pursued him, killed him and married the girl.

"These cowboy films sold like hot cakes, and made a lot of money for us. It was excellent business. We regularly sold between fifty and sixty copies. Each film cost 900 to 1000 dollars, never a penny more. We produced a reel and a half every week, that is four hundred and fifty metres and as we sold only 300 metre reels, we were always ahead. We were always sure of a profit and the money accumulated".

In the summer of 1912 Gaston sailed on the Manuka to Tahiti together with his new young wife, a cameraman and a writer called Edmund Mitchell. On board the ship they shot a comedy *Mr Pott and Mrs Pott*. Arriving in Tahiti and winning the support of Governor Giraud, they made a historical film, *A Ballad of the South Seas*, acted by Maoris. This was the start of a long Pacific filmmaking expedition. Sailing on to Bora Bora by yacht, they shot a further film there, then moved on to New Zealand where they filmed *Ponga (The Kiss)* and *Loved by a Maori Chieftain*. In Australia they made several documentaries about Aboriginals. They made documentaries in Java about the temple of Boro-Boudour; in Indo-China about the ruins of Angkor; and in Cambodia about the royal dancers. Finally in Japan, using non-professional actors, they shot a drama, *The Yellow Slave* – the story of a woman forced into prostitution who commits suicide with her fiancé.

The party returned from the expedition to find that a large part of the film had been ruined by the tropical conditions and bad processing. Such documentary material as was salvaged proved unsaleable. The loss seems to have been the end of the New York branch. Already sick, Gaston returned to France where he died in 1915. The whole affair seems to have ended in some bitterness. In 1944 Méliès' widow said "He had sent his brother as manager of the American branch. I told him: 'Don't trust your brother. He will ruin you. Take a stranger, and if he doesn't do his job, just kick his ass and throw him out'. He didn't listen. Gaston sold everything to Vitagraph and got away with the money. We never saw that money again . . .his brother wanted to make films by himself. They were all terrible"(y).

Some rediscovered examples of Gaston Méliès films shown at the Pordenone Silent Film Days in the late 1980s seemed to confirm the indifferent reputation of American Méliès production.

On 3 May 1913 Georges Méliès' first wife, Eugénie, died. His troubles now seemed to have no end. With the start of the First World War, Parisian theatres, the Robert-Houdin among them, were closed. With production ended and desperate for any means of livelihood, in 1914 Méliès converted a building on the Montreuil property into a little theatre which he called "Variétés Artistique". Leading his repertory company were his daughter, Georgette and her husband, his son André (whose charm and skill as actor can be seen in Georges Franju's *Le Grand Méliès*, in which he plays his own father) and André's wife. Méliès claimed that he himself played 98 roles in the seven years of the theatre, from 1914 to 1923. He was still proud of his variety: the little Variétés Artistiques, he said, performed "all the masterpieces taken from the repertoires of the opera, the opéra-comique, operetta and many dramas, vaudevilles and comedies"(c).

The theatre however did not prosper: "costs in general were too high, with singers, chorus, actors, taxes, authors' rights etc., and above all the theatre was too small to be able to profit even from good audiences"(c). Meanwhile the expenses of maintaining his various properties, which were bringing in no income, increased his debts. There were moratoria; but, according to Méliès, he was mercilessly pursued by an individual creditor (probably he meant Pathé), who succeeded in getting an order for the compulsory sale of all Méliès' Montreuil property. He was ruined and forced to leave the family estate where he had spent his entire life, and created his studio. He had to watch the tools and products of years of work taken off by junk dealers, and the dispersal of "the most unmanageable and baroque objects, of which only the stores of the Châtelet might

Méliès' Studio in ruins

give some idea: aeroplanes, balloons, dirigibles, trams, cars, railways, locomotives, staircases and practicables, props, timber, furnishings of all periods, in short, everything that could be imagined . . . This mass of material came from the fact that Méliès was the first to build, in his films, gigantic constructions, in wood covered with cloth and canvas, and decorated to represent rocks, glaciers, grottoes, infernal or celestial abodes, in which locomotives, motor cars or other vehicles were, in his films, victims of the most burlesque and the most fantastic accidents". Even the theatre of the Variétés Artistiques – his last resort financially speaking – was taken from him. After the Méliès family left in 1923 the property was sold off in lots, though the studio survived, in a progressive state of ruin, until 1945.

At the very same moment that the estate was sold, the Théâtre Robert-Houdin and the Passage

Les Farces du la Lune ou Les Mésaventures de Nostradamus, 1891

de l'Opéra were demolished to make way for the new Boulevard Haussmann. Méliès discovered that his original contract with the Robert-Houdin family obliged him to pay over two thirds of the compensation for expropriation. Obliged to remove the vast accumulation of material

from the theatre and from the premises in Passage de l'Opéra, he now had no place to store it. Several huge crates contained the negatives of all the films he had made between 1896 and 1913. "In a moment of anger and exasperation, he ordered the destruction of all this precious material"(c).

In the hard succeeding years, Méliès found work entertaining in sea-side Casinos, performing operetta or monologues, or conjuring. In the winter he toured in the provinces. In 1924 he was commissioned to refit a theatre in Saarbucken which had been destroyed during the German retreat. This job, in which he was assisted by his son André, occupied him for five months.

On his return to Paris in 1925 he remarried. His new wife, a widow, Charlotte-Stephanie Faes, also known as Fanny Manieux, had performed in the Théâtre Robert-Houdin, under her stage name of Jehanne d'Alcy, from the time Méliès reopened it in 1888. Later she had become his mistress, and appeared in some of his saucier films, such as *Après le Bal – Le Tub*. She too had lost everything she possessed as a result of the war. It seems however that Fanny was the concessionaire of the little toy shop on the Gare Montparnasse which now became the couple's only source of income. Méliès tended the shop for seven years, from 1925 to 1932. "It was, perhaps, the most painful period of his existence, the shop having

Jehanne d'Alcy, Après le bal – Le Tub, 1897

Programme for the Gala Méliès,
1929

Georges Méliès et Carl
Laemmle in 1935 at a banquet
held by the MPPEA

obligatorily to remain open every day from seven in the morning until ten at night. Forbidden to leave it, even for meals, no Sunday, no evening off. In short, prison for a man who till then had been used to absolute liberty. This shop, exposed to all the winds, in an open yard, icy in winter, torrid in summer, was, for a man already old, a true martyrdom. Alas! he had no choice and it was necessary to live, cost what it would"(c).

According to Méliès' own account (which may be a little dramatised) everyone believed him dead until Leon Druhot, who ran the magazine *Ciné-Journal*, discovered him by chance in his little kiosk one day in 1926, and began to publicise the disgraceful plight of this great pioneer of the French cinema. Méliès became a celebrity once more. Reporters hurried to the Gare Montparnasse to interview him.

In 1929 J-P. Mauclair, who ran an avant-garde cinema, came across a cache of old Méliès films, in poor condition, the perforations irreparably torn. Copied and coloured, they thrilled a new generation. On 16 December 1929 a special Gala Méliès was given at the Salle Pleyel. Alongside Cecil B.DeMille's 1915 feature *The Cheat*, with Sessue Hayakawa and Fannie Ward, was shown a group of Méliès films. The theatre was full and the audience ecstatic. Méliès remembered it as one of the most wonderful moments of his life, "in the midst of enthusiastic ovations and a crazy gaiety aroused by the

Méliès in the shop on the Gare
Montparnasse

films, so different from what one sees today . . . The professionals were dumbfounded that it had been possible thirty years ago to make films with rudimentary equipment so perfect, so complicated, remarkable in technique and whose hand-colouring was ravishing". Madame Thuillier, who had run the factory where the colouring had been done by some 200 women workers, came from her retirement home in the country to share the ovation.

Méliès continued to be fêted. More practically he was given a pension – although for three more years he was confined to the little kiosk on the Gare Montparnasse. In 1932 he was given a three-room apartment in the Château d'Orly, where the Mutuelle du Cinéma had just opened a home for veterans of the profession. The Méliès' were the first occupants, and for a while had the château and its beautiful estate to themselves. Méliès and his wife were accompanied by their granddaughter Madeleine, then eight years old. Madeleine, a highly intelligent child whom Méliès

Méliès in the shop on the Gare Montparnasse

adored, was the daughter of Georgette Méliès, whose death in 1930 at the age of 42 was a source of lasting grief to Méliès. She had married an actor Fontaine Fix and herself pursued a career as a singer.

Méliès' last years were serene. His many visitors found him cheerful and not in the least embittered. He drew endlessly, often recreating on paper the scenes and the tricks of his old films. In 1935-6 he took part in two publicity films, though some others which he planned were not made. He was visited and interviewed by journalists, historians and the young co-founder of the Cinémathèque Française, Henri Langlois.

After making a radio broadcast in December 1937 Méliès became ill and was taken to the Hôpital Léon-Bellan. There, on 21 January 1938 he died. He was buried in the family vault in the cemetery of Père-Lachaise. Fanny Méliès, known as Jehanne d'Alcy, survived him by eighteen years.

Méliès' tomb in the Père-Lachaise cemetery

6
G. MÉLIÈS
LEGACY

When Méliès died only a handful of his films – the little cache that was shown at the 1929 Méliès Gala – had been recovered from the debris of film history. Since then the advent of film archives has salvaged more, and the dedicated work of his granddaughter and great-grandson has so far assembled a body of more than 150 films out of the original total of over 500. The proportion is far better than for most of Méliès' contemporaries, even if it cannot ever compensate for the wilful destruction of 1923.

Méliès' place in film history is secure. He was the first to show the potential of the film as narrative and spectacle, and to explore almost every genre. He created the basic vocabulary of special effects. He established the pattern of studio practice that was to persist throughout most of the silent period. The extraordinary and universal attraction of his films for the early-century audience did much to establish an international market for the cinema, and to promote the supremacy of the French film industry at that time.

Yet Méliès does not merely inhabit a niche in history. He is the earliest filmmaker whose work still survives on its own merits and with its own personality. The test of his true artistry is that he was inimitable. In his own day he was persistently copied and plagiarised by other film makers; but the imitations, however ingenious, can never for a moment be mistaken for the original. Every aspect was so marked with style that a single frame by Méliès is instantly recognisable.

Seeing a Méliès film today, our response to the fun, the vitality, the trickery, the story, the décor is still very much what was intended, almost a hundred years ago. When Méliès the magician addresses us, in gestures from his proscenium-screen, we are drawn in, accomplices with him. The visions he created are part of the common cinematic consciousness – or, more correctly, subconscious, for he created a world of dreams and the imagination.

Méliès' universe is full of miracles and nonsense. It looks backwards to Lewis Carroll and forward to the delirious irrationality of the Surrealists, who understood and loved Méliès – even though he was baffled when they claimed him as a 'poet', which he thought was strictly a pen and ink trade.

La légende de Rip Van Winckle, 1905

Nothing in his world is what it seems. In an instant, objects turn into people, butterflies metamorphose into chorus beauties, men become women, anyone may vanish in a puff of smoke. Limbs and heads become detached, and go on about their normal business amiably unconcerned until they eventually find their way back to their rightful locations. Boxes and chests and cupboards are natural marvels, which can devour or disgorge any quantity of bags of gold or devils or pretty girls. Travellers forever risk putting up in haunted hotels where the furniture has an inconvenient life of its own and the food is all Tantalus frustration. Méliès despatches his heroes, by land and air, over the sea and under it, on quests and odysseys of endless fantasy.

All this came out of Méliès' imagination and was contained on his six-metre stage. He painted his settings and props, designed his costumes, directed everything. The visual style is his and his alone, without

Le Royaume des Fées, 1903

comparison. His creation is as personal, as distinctive and as haunting as that of Douanier Rousseau, Chagall or Bosch; and its originality is not diminished by its origins in the kitsch and popular arts of the *Belle Epoque* or its single intention to entertain a fairground audience. More than sixty years ago the critic André Mauge admirably summed up Méliès' unique achievement and legacy: "Today's film makers have to struggle for even relative independence. Méliès did what he wished. That is why despite the years his work retains such a marvellous innocence, a purity which has been lost and will never be found again. He showed in his films, with the means available to him, precisely what his genius dictated."

NOTES

(Notes with alphabetical indications refer to the Bibliography)

(1)   Jones and Co were outfitters and military tailors. Méliès' biographers have passed down colourful anecdotes about his blushing sales of corsets to ladies.

(2)   Robert-Houdin in *Memoirs of Robert-Houdin, Ambassador, Author, and Conjuror*. London, Chapman and Hall, 1860.

(3)   The programme printed on a leaflet that was current in the second week of 1896 consists of: 1. *La Sortie de l'Usine LUMIERE a Lyon*, 2. *La Voltige*, 3. *La Peche aux Poissons Rouges*, 4. *Le Débarquement du Congrès de Photographie à Lyon*, 5. *Les Forgerons*, 6. *Le Jardinier*, 7. *Le Repas*, 8. *Le Saut à la Couverture*, 9. *La Place des Cordeliers à Lyon*, 10. *La Mer*.

(4)   An alternative version of Antoine Lumière's refusal is quoted in Maurice Bessy and Lo Duca's *Georges Méliès*: "Young man, thank me. This invention is not for sale, but for you, it would be ruin. It can be exploited for a while as a scientific curiosity; beyond that it has no commercial future". This version, whose touch of altruism is more flattering to Antoine, was related to Lo Duca by Lumière, who was not himself present at the time. Méliès' first-hand recollection seems more credible.

(5)   There is some uncertainty about the precise date on which R.W.Paul's Theatrograph was put on the market. John Barnes, in *The Beginnings of the Cinema in England* (1976), suggests that the original Theatrograph had shortcomings and, though used for some theatrical demonstrations, was quickly replaced by a new model, patented on March 2 1896. The American conjuror Carl Hertz claimed that he had with difficulty persuaded Paul to part with what seems to have been the prototype of the new production model, in order to have it before he sailed for South Africa on March 28. By 25 April however *The Era* described Paul as "a manufacturer of 'graph machines at eighty pounds apiece". The likeliest time for Méliès' purchase then is some time during April 1896.

(6)   In September 1897 appeared a brochure by Georges Brunel in a series about current projection devices: *Les projections animées: Le Kinétograph Méliès et Reulos*.

(7)   "On August 28 [1895] *The execution of Mary Queen of Scots* was taken under the management of Alfred Clark . . . it contains the earliest example we know of 'stop motion'. This was possibly the idea of Clark, and this in spite of many claims for Georges Méliès, who did not touch a motion picture camera until months later. The part of Mary was played by R.I.Thomae, secretary and treasurer of the Kinetoscope Company. Thomae places his head on the block, the camera is stopped, a dummy substituted, the camera started again, and the head of the dummy chopped off" (Gordon Hendricks: *The Kinetoscope* (New York, 1966).

(8)   Although Méliès had shot several films in the Place de l'Opéra before *Escamotage d'une Dame*, the French historian Georges Sadoul questioned whether the incident which Méliès described had actually taken place as early as 1896, since not until 1898 (at the same time that the Méliès catalogue advertises a new view of the Place de l'Opéra) does the description "scene à transformation" begin to appear regularly in the catalogue. However the titles of many films of 1896 and 1897 now lost suggest that they may have included stop-action effects; and moreoever it seems improbable that in relating his story Méliès would have forgotten the chronology of his first important disappearance film.

(9)   The Star-Film catalogues advertise "Offices in London, Paris, Barcelona, New York".

(10)   Méliès' sets were painted in monochrome: colours photographed unpredictably on the early film emulsions.

(11)   From Méliès' answer to a questionnaaire, 1930.

BIBLIOGRAPHY

(a)   Georges Méliès: *Les Vues Cinématographiques. In Annuaire General et International de la photographie*. Paris, 1907.

(b)   Georges Méliès: *En Marge de l'Histoire du Cinématographe in Ciné-Journal, Le Journal du Film*. Paris, 1926.

(c)   Georges Méliès: *Mes Memoires*. Rome, 1938, reprinted in (d).

(d)   Maurice Bessy, G.M.Lo Duca: *Georges Méliès, Mage*. Paris, Prisma, 1945/Paris, J.J.Pauvert, 1961.

(e)   Georges Sadoul: *An Index to the Creative Work of Georges Méliès*. London, British Film Institute, 1947.

(f)   *Exposition Commemorative du Centenaire de Georges Méliès* (catalogue). Paris, Cinémathèque Francaise/Union Centrale des Arts Decoratifs, 1961.

(g)   Madeleine Malthête-Méliès: *Georges Méliès, Createur du Spectacle Cinématographique*. Paris, privately printed, 1961, 2nd ed. 1966.

(h)   Georges Sadoul: *Georges Méliès*. Paris, Editions Seghers, 1962.

(i)   Jacques Deslandes: *Le Boulevard du Cinéma à l'epoque de Georges Méliès*. Paris, Editions du Crrf, 1963.

(j)   *Petit Festival Georges Méliès* Vienna, Oestereichisches Filmuseum, 1964.

(k)   Maurice Bessy: *Méliès*. Paris, Anthologie du Cinema, 1966.

(l)   Jacques Deslandes, Jacques Richard: *Histoire comparée du cinéma*, tome II. Paris, Casterman, 1968.

(m)   Gérard Lenne: *Le Cinéma fantastique et ses mythologies*. Paris, Editions du Cerf, 1970.

(n)   Madeleine Malthête-Méliès: *Méliès l'Enchanteur*. Paris, Hachette, 1973. Revised edition, Paris, Malthete-Méliès, 1985.

(o)   Paul Hammond: *Marvellous Méliès*. London, Gordon Fraser, 1974.

(p)   John Frazer: *Artificially Arranged Scenes: The Films of Georges Méliès*. Boston, G.K.Hall, 1979.

(q)   Jacques Malthête-Méliès (ed.): *Essai de reconstitution du catalogue francais de la Star-Film*. Paris, CNC, 1981.

(r)   Paolo Cerchi-Usai: *Georges Méliès*. Florence, La Nuova Italia, 1983.

(s)   *158 Scenarios de Films Disparus de Georges Méliès*. Paris, Association "les Amis de Georges Méliès", 1986.

(t)   *Dal Teatro al Cinema: Georges Méliès*. Trieste, Club Rosselli, 1988.

(u)   Paolo Cerchi-Usai (ed.) *Lo Schermo Incantato/A Trip to the Movies*. Rochester/Pordenone, George Eastman House/Edizione Biblioteca dell'Immagine/Giornate del Cinema Muto, 1991.

(v)   Star-Film Catalogues. Paris, New York, various dates.

(w)   Warwick Film Catalogues, various dates.

(x)   Charles Urban Trading Company catalogues.

(y)   Bulletin of the Association "les Amis de Georges Méliès", 1982 -.

MELIES CHRONOLOGY

NOTE: This chronology cites only a selection of the most significant of Méliès' film productions. The full catalogue is too extensive to be included in the scope of this book. For comprehensive listing of Méliès filmographies see in the Bibliography (d), (e), (f), (h), (j), (n), (o), (p), (q), (r). To date the CNC Essai de rconstitution du catalogue francais de la Star-Film (q; new edition due in 1993) supplemented by (s), provides the most reliable and comprehensive.

1815 Birth of Jean-Stanislas-Louis Méliès, father of Georges, at Lavelanet (Ariege).

1818 Birth of Johannah Catherine Schuering, mother of Georges, at Schweninge, Holland.

1845 Robert-Houdin (1805-1871) establishes theatre in the Palais-Royal. J-S-L. Méliès marries Johannah-Catherine Schuering.

1847 Jean-Stanislas-Louis Méliès establishes shoe factory at 29 Boulevard Saint-Martin; later at 36 rue Meslay, 57 rue Taylor.

1844 Birth of Henri Méliès.

1852 12 February. Birth of Gaston Méliès.

1853 (or 1854). Théâtre Robert-Houdin moves from Palais-Royal to 8, Boulevard des Italiens.

1859 Méliès factory established at 29 Boulevard Saint-Martin.

1861 8 December. Birth of Georges Méliès.

1865 20 March. Birth of Charlotte Faes, known as Fanny Manieux, Jehanne d'Alcy, eventually Méliès' second wife.

1868 Méliès enrolled in Lycée du Prince Imperial, Vanves.

1870 Franco-Prussian War: Méliès' lycée transferred to Lycée Louis-le-Grand.

1873 Henri Méliès joins family business.

1878 Gaston Méliès joins family business.

1880 20 July. Méliès attains baccalauréat.

1881 12 November. Méliès enrols for military service in 113rd Regiment of Infantry at Blois (Loir-et-Cher). His army records describe him as 1m. 72 tall, blonde, with blue eyes.

1882 12 November. Discharge from military service with rank of corporal. Begins work in parental factory.

1884 Méliès spends most of year in London, working in outfitter's shop and amusing himself with visits to theatres and Egyptian Hall.

1885 29 June. Marries Eugénie Genin, who brings him a dowry of 50,000F. The couple move into an apartment on the fifth floor of the family building, 5, rue Taylor.

1888 J-S-L.Méliès retires to Niort, handing over running of factory to sons Henri and Gaston.
February. Birth of Méliès' daughter, Georgette.
1 July. Méliès becomes director of Théâtre Robert-Houdin, on first floor of 8, Boulevard des Italiens, which he has bought with his share of the family business. Announcements of shows under the new management begin to appear in October.
12 December. Méliès presents his first important illusion *La Stroubaika Persane*.

1889 Méliès contributes cartoons, signed "Geo Smile", to the anti-Boulangiste magazine *La Griffe*, directed by his cousin Adolphe Méliès.
11 October. Presents illusion *L'Orchestre*.
13 October. Presents illusion *Le Fée des Fleurs, ou le Miroir de Cagliostro*.
19 December. Presents illusion *L'Enchanteur Alcofrisbas*.

1890 10 January. Presents illusion *Le Valet de Trefle vivant*.
March. Presents the illusion *Hypnotisme, Catalepsie, magnetisme*.
September. Presents illusion *Le Manoir du Diable*.
December. Presents illusion *Le Nain jaune*.

1891 Méliès establishes l'Academie de Prestidigitation.
March. Presents illusion *American spritualistic Mediums, ou Le Décapité récalcitrant*.
July. Presents illusion *Les Farces de la Lune ou Les Mésaventures de Nostradamus*.
December. Presents illusion *Le Calif de Bagdad*.

1892 June. Presents illusion *Le Charlatan fin de siècle*.
October. Presents illusion *La Source enchantée*.
December. Presents illusion *Le Dai Kang*.

1893 December. Presents illusions *La Caverne des Gnomes* (in foyer of theatre), *Isis*, *L'Escarpolette Polonaise*.

1894 May. Presents illusion *L'Auberge du Diable*.
December. Presents illusion *Le Château de Mesmer*.

1895 October. Presents illusion *Le Rêve de Coppelius* (in foyer of theatre).
December. Presents illusion *Thomas Oldboot*.
Antoine Lumière rents photographic studio over Théâtre Robert-Houdin.
28 December. First show of Lumière Cinématographe at Grand Café, Boulevard des Capucines. Méliès is among invited audience.

1896 January. Presents illusion *Le Pilori*.
February. Presents illusion *Le Miracle du Brahmine*.
April. Méliès purchases projector from Robert William Paul in London.
April (?) With aid of Reulos makes rudimentary camera. Buys unperforated Eastman stock in London; perforates it with machine commissioned from Lapipe.
March. Presents illusion *Les Rayons Roentgen*.
4 April – July 1896. Edison films projected at Théâtre Robert-Houdin.
May. Méliès photographs first film, *Une Partie de Cartes*, followed by 25 other subjects. Méliès photographs films during holidays in region of Trouville.

August. With reopening of theatre, Méliès first advertises films and apparatus for sale.

2 September. Méliès patents Kinétographe Robert-Houdin.

20 December. Star trade mark first used in advertising.

December. Presents stage illusion *Le Mystère de Memphis, ou La Resurrection de Cleopatre*.

During the year Méliès photographs 78 short films (numbered 1-80 in his catalogue: a catalogue number is given to each 20m. roll, even though some titles, such as 78-90, *The Haunted Castle*, may be made up of several rolls, each individually numbered). The films include: *Arrivée d'un Train* (7), *Panorama d'Havre, pris d'un bateau* (34), *Danse Serpentine* (44), *Cortège du Tsar, Bois de Boulogne* (50), *Dessinateur: Chamberlain* (57), *Escamotage d'une Dame chez Robert-Houdin* (70), *Tom Oldboots* (75), *Le Manoir du Diable* (78-80).

897 January. Presents stage illusion *La Cage d'Or*.

Méliès constructs studio at Montreuil.

Publication of descriptive pamphlet on the Kinétographe.

4 May. Conflagration of the Bazar de la Charité results in many deaths and damages reputation and popularity of cinema shows.

2 September. Méliès abandons live shows for films in the evening performances at Théâtre Robert Houdin.

Méliès produces 54 titles (catalogue numbers 81-137), including three films of the café-chantant singer Paulus, shot by electric light in the Théâtre Robert-Houdin (88-90); Méliès' first reconstituted actualities *Episodes de Guerre* (103-110); also *Le Cabinet de Mephistopheles* (118-120), *L'Auberge Ensorcelée* (122-123), *Après le Bal, le Tub* (128).

At end of year Méliès ends association with Reulos.

898 Death of Jean-Stanislas-Louis Méliès.

Méliès produces 31 titles (catalogue numbers 138-171), including *Faust et Marguerite* (138), *Magie Diabolique Georges Méliès* (140-141), *Les Rayons Roentgen* (142), *Visite sous-marine du "Maine"* (147), *Combat Navale devant Manille* (150), *Damnation de Faust* (158), *La Lune à un Mètre* (160-162), *L'Homme de Têtes* (167), *La Tentation de Saint Antoine* (169).

Apparently during the course of this year Méliès erects an open-air screen outside Théâtre Robert-Houdin to show publicity films both for products and for his own theatre.

Méliès equips a laboratory in Passage de l'Opéra and engages Lallemant to do the printing.

899 16 April. Magic revue *Passez Muscade* at Théâtre Robert-Houdin incorporates films.

November. Death of Méliès' mother.

Méliès produces 34 films (catalogue numbers 173-231) including *Le Diable au Couvent* (185-187), *Le Christ marchant sur les Eaux* (204), *L'Affaire Dreyfus* (206-217) *Cendrillon* (219-224), *Le Chevalier Mystère* (226-227), *L'Homme Protée* (228).

Alteration and enlargement of studio.

900 Méliès produces 31 films (catalogue numbers 232-315), including a group of scenes of the Exposition Universelle of 1900 (245-261), *L'Homme Orchestre* (262-263), *Jeanne d''Arc* (264-276), *Rêve de Noël* (298-305).

1901 1 January. Fire – starting in photographic studio above – partially destroys Théâtre Robert-Houdin. Méliès redesigns the decor in rococo style.

15 January. Birth of André Méliès.

Méliès produces 27 films (catalogue numbers 316-378) including *Le Brahmane et le Papillon* (332-333), *Dislocation Mystérieuse* (335-336), *Le Petit Chaperon Rouge* (337-344), *L'Omnibus des Toques ou Les Echappes de Charenton* (359), *Barbe-Bleue* (361-370).

During this year Méliès' cameraman Leclerc, arrested for selling pornographic photographs, is replaced by Michaut.

1902 Méliès produces 22 films (catalogue numbers 379-443), including *Le Bataillon Elastique* (381), *L'Homme à la Tête de Caoutchouc* (382), *Le Diable Géant. Le Miracle de la Madone ou Le Diable et la Statue* (384-385), *Nain et Géant* (386), *L'Armoire des Frères Davenport* (387-389), *Eruption Volcanique à la Martinique* (397), *Catastrophe du ballon "Pax"* (398), *Voyage dans la Lune* (399-411), *Le Sacre d'Edouard VII* (no catalogue number), *L'Homme Mouche* (415-416), *La Femme Volante* (417-418), *Chirurgie Fin de Siècle, ou Une Indigestion* (422-427), *Voyages de Gulliver* (426-429), *Robinson Crusoe* (430-443).

1903 Méliès opens Star-Film agency at 204 East 38th St, New York. Gaston Méliès, having suffered misfortunes in the boot business as a result of an army contract, is sent to take charge of the agency.

Méliès begins to deposit paper prints of films with Library of Congress, Washington for copyright purposes.

Méliès produces 29 films (catalogue numbers 444-533), including *Le Mélomane* (479-480), *Le Royaume des Fées* (483-498), *L'Enchanteur Alcofribas* (514-516), *La Lanterne Magique* (520-524), *Faust aux Enfers ou La Damnation de Faust* (527-533). The opera films are sold with accompanying musical scores.

Méliès' employees Michaut, Astaix and Lallemand leave to form the rental concern American Kinema. Méliès engages Tainguy as cameraman.

1904 24 May. Méliès elected President of newly-formed Chambre Syndicale de la Prestidigitation.

1905 Méliès presents new illusion, *Le Nouveau miracle du Brahmin*, in Théâtre Robert-Houdin.

Méliès produces 45 films (catalogue numbers 534-667) including *Au Clair de la Lune ou Pierrot Malheureux* (538-539), *Damnation du Dr Faust* (561-574), *Le Merveilleux Eventail Vivant* (581-582), *Le Barbier de Seville* (606-625), *Voyage à travers l'Impossible* (649-659), *Le Juif Errant* (662-664).

1905 Méliès produces 12 films (catalogue numbers 668-785) including *L'Ange de Noël* (669-677), *Les Cartes Vivantes* (678-679), *Le Banquet de Messmer* (693-695), *Le Palais des mille et une Nuits* (705-726), *La Tour de Londres et les Derniers Moments d'Anne de Boleyn* (732-737), *Le Raid Paris-Monte Carlo en deux heures* (740-749), *La légende de Rip Van Winckle* (756-765).

Méliès installs electric scene lighting and a printing laboratory at Montreuil; opens second studio at rue de Pré.

1906 Méliès produces 18 films (catalogue numbers 786-905) including *Jack le Ramoneur* (781-806), *Les Incendiaires* (824-838), *Les quatre cents Farces du Diable* (849-865), *La Fée Carabosse ou Le Poignard Infernal* (877-887), *Robert Macaire et Bertrand, Les Rois des Cambrioleurs* (888-905).

1907 November. Méliès resumes creation of magic tricks for Théâtre Robert-Houdin, with *Osiris* and *Le Diable vert*.
September. Presents "revue retrospective moderne des phénomènes spirites", *Les Phénomènes du Spiritisme*, at Théâtre Robert-Houdin.
Méliès produces 19 films (catalogue numbers 906-1022), including *Deux cents milles lieues sous les mers, ou Le Cauchemar d'un Pêcheur* (912-924), *Le Tunnel sous la Manche ou Le Cauchemar Franco-Anglais* (936-950), *Le Delirium Tremens ou La Fin d'un Alcoolique* (956-960), *Eclipse de Soleil en Pleine Lune* (961-968), *Hamlet, Prince de Danemark* (980-987), *Shakespeare: La Mort de Julius Caesar* (995-999).

1908 Gaston Méliès establishes American Star-Film Company in Chicago, to produce films, with capital of $75,000.
18 December. Gaston Méliès joins Edison trust.
Méliès produces 45 films (catalogue numbers 1023-1441) including *La Civilisation à travers les Ages* (1050-1069), *La Photographie Electrique à Distance* (1091-1095), *Le Raid Paris-New York en Automobile* (from this title onwards not all Méliès films have catalogue numbers), *Conte de la Grandmère et Rêve de l'Enfant/Au Pays des Jouets* (1314-1325), *La Fée Libellule* (1372-1385).

1909 2-4 July. Méliès presides at Congrès International des Fabricants de Films, at which it is resolved to cease selling films in favour of renting.
Méliès produces *Phènomènes de Spiritisme* for Folies-Bergere.
Although the dating of Méliès' films after 1908 presents some problems, he appears to have produced 9 films in 1909 (no catalogue numbers).

1910 Méliès produces approximately 15 films during this year (among them catalogue numbers 1476-1533) including *Le Locataire diabolique* (1495-1501).
Méliès produces *Les Fantômes du Nile* at the Alhambra and Olympia, Paris; and then on tour.
Beween 1910 and 1912 Gaston Méliès makes approximtely 135 Westerm films in Texas and California.

1911 Méliès resumes production, but distributes through Pathé. He produces only two films: *Les Hallucinations de Baron Munchausen, Le Vitrail diabolique*.
Gaston Méliès production adopts name of American Wild West and sets up headquarters at Santa Paula.

1912 Méliès produces his last four films: *A la Conquête du Pôle, Cendrillon, ou la Pantoufle Mystérieuse, Le Chevalier des Neiges, Le Voyage de la famille Bourrichon*.
July – December. Gaston Méliès embarks on Pacific tour, resulting in approximtely 32 titles.

1913 Méliès, having definitively given up film production returns to direction of Théâtre Robert-Houdin.
3 May. Death of Eugénie Méliès.
Gaston Méliès continues to film throughout Pacific region. The film however proves to be mostly spoilt as a result of high temperatures.

1914 Gaston Méliès ceases production in United States; and, discouraged and ill, returns to France.
August. On outbreak of First World War, Théâtre Robert-Houdin is closed along with other Parisian theatres.

1915 In early summer Théâtre Robert-Houdin reopens, but poor business forces Méliès to sub-let theatre to a cinema exhibitor.
Méliès opens his Théâtre des Variétés Artistiques at Montreuil.
Death of Gaston Méliès in Corsica, following sea-food poisoning.

1920 Resumption of meetings of Chambre Syndicale de la Prestidigitation.

1923 Demolition of Théâtre Robert-Houdin and Passage de l'Opéra.
Méliès is obliged through financial failure to give up his Montreuil property.

1924 Méliès goes to Saarbrucken to restore the Grand Théâtre du Cercle des Mines.

1925 Méliès lives at 107, rue Lafayette.
December. Marries Charlotte Faes, known as Jehanne d'Alcy. Méliès begins to work in his wife's boutique on the Gare Montparnasse.
Leon Coissac publishes Méliès' memoirs in his *Histoire du Cinéma*.

1928 Leon Druhot, editor of *Ciné-Journal*, alerts journalists to Méliès' situation.

1929 October. Special Méliès issue of *La Révue du Cinéma*.
16 December. Gala Méliès at Salle Pleyel, Paris.

1930 Death of Georgette Méliès-Fix, daughter of Méliès.

1931 Méliès decorated with Croix de la Legion d'Honneur, by Louis Lumière.

1932 September. Méliès and his wife and grand-daughter Madeleine are given three-room apartment in Château d'Orly, owned by the Mutuelle du Cinéma.

1935/6 Méliès makes two publicity films and scripts others which are not realised.

1937 Méliès became ill after making a broadcast.

1938 21 January. Death of Georges Méliès in Hôpital Leopold-Bellan.
25 January. Méliès is buried in the family vault in Père-Lachaise, after a service at the church of Notre-Dame-du-Travail, rue Veringétorix, Paris.

1956 Death of Madame Georges Méliès at Versailles.

1961 Méliès centenary commemorated by exhibition organised by Cinémathèque Française, at the Musée des Arts Decoratifs, Palais du Louvre.

1980 Farewell performance of André Méliès, in *Land of Smiles* at the Casino d'Enghien.

1981 Cinémathèque Francaise celebrates 80th birthday of André Méliès.

1985 1 March. Death of André Méliès.